Here You Are at Wayne Community College
Success Ahead!

Third Edition

Rosalyn F. Lomax
Wayne Community College

KENDALL/HUNT PUBLISHING COMPANY
4050 Westmark Drive   Dubuque, Iowa 52002

Pages 33–34: "The Week That Was" Your Current Time Schedule is used with permission from
Funk et al: Thrills, Spills, and Study Skills. Copyright © 1992 Kendall/Hunt Publishing Company.

Front cover photos by Malcolm Shearin, Wayne Community College Media Dept.
Back cover photo by the author.

ISBN 0-7872-8686-9

Printed in the United States of America
10 9 8 7 6 5 4 3 2 1

Author's Acknowledgments

To all the students who made me care enough to write a book;

To all the volunteer ACA 111 instructors at WCC (and the volunteer Study Skills instructors including Ann Spicer, who developed the study skills course for the orientation program);

To a supportive administration at WCC including Dr. Ed Wilson, especially for his commitment to visiting the evening ACA 111 classes every semester; Curtis Shivar (retired) for always being beside me (and often far ahead of me leading the way) on orientation concerns; and George Fouts (now at GTCC) for approving this project;

To faculty and staff who advised and consulted on the various sections of this book and those who served on the special 1993 committee whose recommendations helped strengthen the program, with special thanks to Janice Hill, who was instrumental in creating the original manual and who accompanied me on my earliest ACA 111 journey;

To my closest colleagues (including walking partners and other best friends) who endured my endless queries and requests for ideas and who inspire me perpetually;

To Dr. John Gardner of the University of South Carolina, my hero in the Freshman Year Experience movement, whose program gave my name to an editor looking for potential authors;

To teachers from my past who cared deeply (including Miss Exum, Mrs. Switzer, Dr. Bryant, Dr. Ellis, Dr. Voitle);

To my children, Fleming and Fred, for their love, support, inspiration, and endurance; and to Fred for naming the book;

To my husband, who not only loves, supports, inspires, endures, and brags on his wife, but also transferred this whole project to a WordPerfect 6.0 disk;

And to my parents, who worked very hard to make it very easy for me to succeed in college and who would be very proud if they were alive to see me publish a little textbook;

And to God,

I give thanks.

Contents

To the Student

While I was first working on this textbook in 1995, I attended a conference with eight hundred people from forty-three states as well as Canada, England, China, New Zealand, and Australia. Participants met for four days to talk about a topic all of them are passionately interested in: YOU. The University of South Carolina's National Resource Center for the Freshman Year Experience sponsored the conference for advocates of first-year college students.

Caring deeply about my own students at Wayne Community College is what first drew me to a lecture by Professor John Gardner of the University of South Carolina at a conference in San Francisco several years ago. His recollections of his own first college year and his determination to do all he can to improve that experience for college students today inspired me to become more involved in Wayne Community College's efforts to give new students a good beginning.

Look around this beautiful campus! Hundreds of students like you are starting their college experience; hundreds of others are alive and well after spending a year or more here!

Look again! Faculty members are here because of you. Staff members are here because of you. Administrators are here because of you. The *college* is here because of you. The philosophy, purpose statement, and goals of this college focus on you. In the words of the French, you are the college's *raison d'etre*, its reason for being.

Probably the people you will see most on campus besides other students are your instructors. Please remember something important about them: long ago (and not so very long ago for some) they were college students too. Every instructor here had a first day, a first quarter or semester, a first year of college. They know what it's like.

How many times have you heard that you are entering one of the most exhilarating periods of your whole life? Well, it's true! College can indeed be one of life's best experiences and can indeed set the tone for the rest of your life. Remember the scene in *Dead Poets Society* where Mr. Keating has the boys listen to the portraits of students from the past? "Seize the day!" is what he wants them to hear. You will be at Wayne Community College a relatively short time before you complete your degree or transfer or reach your short-term goal. *Carpe diem!* (Seize the day!) Put as much into your college experience as you can find within yourself. Take advantage of the many resources on this campus. As one of my English students expressed the philosophy on his poetry test, "Seize the day before it seizes you!"

You are entering an environment where students of diverse ages and backgrounds have blossomed and flourished. One inspiring example is Kwai Chun Lee Chan, a forty-six-year-old native of Hong Kong. She actively involved herself at Wayne Community College as a top student, a work-study student, the International Students' Club founder, an academic honor society Phi Theta Kappa member, and a friend to all she met. Somehow she found time to serve various community agencies as translator. Faculty members Kathryn Spicer and Miriam Wessell nominated her for USA Today's All-American Scholar team. Kwai made the *first* team and earned the Centennial Scholar designation as the top-ranking North Carolinian in the national competition. She was recognized for these national honors in ceremonies in Chicago at the convention of the American Association of Community Colleges with WCC's president, Dr. Ed Wilson.

Kwai is one of many students who have distinguished themselves at WCC and beyond in universities, careers, communities, and families. All of these students "seized the day" at WCC. So can you!

This book addresses some of the concerns and needs of college students everywhere, but it also introduces you to *your* college. May your experience here at Wayne Community College be a challenging and rewarding chapter of a challenging and rewarding life. *Carpe diem* and savor each moment!

Rosalyn Fleming Lomax
English Instructor and Student Sucess Coordinator
Wayne Community College

Chapter One

Welcome to ACA 111

Where have I been? Where am I? What am I doing here? What do I know about college? What do I need to know in order to survive in college and to succeed in college? What must I do to become who and what I want to become?

ACA is the prefix assigned by the North Carolina Community College System to identify courses *related* to your *academic* requirements (academic related). ACA 111, College Student Success, is a graduation requirement in all curriculum programs at Wayne Community College. It is recommended for all students, preferably in their first semester on campus. Most sections of the one credit hour course meet twice weekly until midterm. Grading is by Pass/Fail.

Instructors determine their own assignments and testing, but one basic requirement is attendance at thirteen of the sixteen scheduled class meetings. This requirement reflects the college's attendance policy which appears in short form in your *Student Handbook* and with additional explanation in your *General Catalog*. The college views class attendance as an essential and as a student's responsibility. A student whose absences exceed twenty percent of the scheduled class hours cannot receive credit for the course. Thus ACA 111 students must attend at least thirteen of their sixteen hours of class to receive credit.

Most colleges and universities have a course like this called by various names such as College Survival Skills, Freshman Seminar, Orientation, Student Success, College 101, or University 101. Whatever the name, whatever the credit, whatever the requirements, whatever the grading system, all the courses have a common goal: to make the beginning of college a good experience for students.

Instructors in the orientation courses at most schools are volunteers. They teach the course in addition to their regular duties or course loads. Obviously they care about what happens to new students. ACA 111 instructors at Wayne Community College are volunteers who want you to feel comfortable consulting them both in class and at their offices whenever you need assistance. Your individual ACA 111 instructor represents another resource person for you on this campus in addition to your academic advisor, your regular instructors, and other staff members. Please keep your ACA 111 instructor on your mental list of people you can turn to even after this course has ended.

The other students in your class are another resource for you in this course. You will probably have several opportunities to get to know each other with no academic pressure involved; the very first class meeting will probably find you doing some rather informal activity unlike what you anticipated doing in college. Relax and have some fun getting to know the other students. Most of them are new here like you; if a few have been on campus for a while and are just now taking the course, consider them as resource people who know the ropes already. (Your instructor will also welcome ideas from these experienced students to help enhance your first semester here.) You may be in other classes with some of these same students; familiar faces can look good. Many students develop study groups early in their careers here, and ACA 111 is a good place to start discovering who shares your learning style, study preferences, and required courses.

One student wrote this comment on the evaluation form at the end of the course: "This class gave me a sense of belonging. Without it I might have given up." That is one of the main reasons for the course. Some students in community colleges may indeed feel isolated. Being first-generation college students in their families or peer groups, having commitments as employees and parents, and lacking opportunities for interaction with classmates beyond the classroom—these and other circumstances increase feelings of isolation (Barkley 2). An hour of credit toward graduation is the official reward for taking the course, but a sense of belonging, of being part of a community, may be a much more significant reward.

In ACA 111 you will hear a number of speakers including your instructor. They will provide important information on topics like study skills, financial aid, admissions and records details, health issues, motivation and self-esteem, time management and goal setting, and career and transfer information. You may take a short form of a personality profile that will help you determine or confirm your college and career plans. You will tour the library and the academic assistance facilities like the Academic Skills Center, the Writing Center, and the Basic Skills Computer Lab.

From every speaker and tour, you will be developing a file of familiar faces, voices, and places that will be easier to find when you need them later because of your exposure to them in this class. Students frequently comment on their evaluations of ACA 111, "I never would have known about _____ if it hadn't been for this class."

Most Sections of this course end around midterm. It would be impossible to tell you *everything* you need to know about college before then, especially in sixteen hours, but a realistic goal of ACA 111 is to help make you aware of what awaits you here and in life.

Many poets have written about the impact of our experiences on our lives; their words remind us that everything we do and everyone we meet will influence what we become. Your college experience, beginning with this course, will become a part of your total person. *Becoming* is the process all of us are involved in—surviving, succeeding, becoming....

WHERE HAVE I BEEN? WHERE AM I?
WHAT AM I DOING HERE?

Consider where you have been, where you are, and why you are here. Consider what you can hope to get out of this class and out of your college experience. Write your thoughts.

WHY AM I HERE?

_____

_____

_____

_____

WHAT DO I HOPE TO GET OUT OF THIS CLASS?

_____

_____

_____

WHAT DO I HOPE TO GET OUT OF MY WCC EXPERIENCE?

_____

_____

_____

_____

WRITE A FEW SENTENCES RESPONDING TO ONE OF THE FOLLOWING QUOTATIONS:

I am a part of all that I have met.

Tennyson, "Ulysses"

[We are . . . strong in will]
To strive, to seek, to find, and not to yield.

Tennyson, "Ulysses"

There was a child went forth every day
And the first object he look'd upon, that object he became,
And that object became part of him for the day or a certain part of the day,
Or for many years or stretching cycles of years.

Whitman, "There Was a Child Went Forth"

RESPONSE:

_____

_____

_____

_____

_____

_____

Chapter Two

Welcome to Wayne Community College

Once upon a time Wayne Community College was known as Goldsboro Industrial Education Center, established June 15, 1957, as one of the original thirteen industrial education centers in the state. Classes for students, all part-time, met at night at Goldsboro High School until 1960 when the first building was completed on the campus at Wayne Memorial Drive and Highway 70. Fall of 1962 brought the first full-time and daytime students to what became Wayne Technical Institute in 1963 and Wayne Community College in 1967. (Meanwhile, three extension units of the original school were growing into Carteret, James Sprunt, and Sampson Community Colleges.) Steady growth produced the need for a larger facility, ultimately the beautiful campus at 3000 Wayne Memorial Drive, YOUR CAMPUS.

Fall of 1996 brought to completion another phase in campus construction. The new Aviation Classroom Building at the Goldsboro-Wayne Municipal Airport opened for Fall Quarter 1996 classes. On the main campus, breezeways at the back of HS and MSS Buildings lead to the two newest classroom buildings, Agriculture and Automotive and Allied Health, which opened in time for Winter Quarter classes in November 1996.

The next building to be constructed is the new Child Care Center south of the south perimeter road across from Holly and Pine Buildings. According to WCC President Ed Wilson, this facility should open by Fall Semester of 2002 and will serve approximately fifty children from toddlers to age four. Early Childhood Education majors will welcome the completion of this project.

The passage of Higher Education Improvement Bonds on November 7, 2000, provided almost $13 million in funds for renovation and additional buildings. Students, faculty, and staff volunteered in a phone-a-thon to inform voters about the bond referendum prior to election day, and Wayne County voters supported the bonds. New construction could begin on the north side of campus during your years at WCC.

Wayne Community College can proudly claim one of the most beautiful facilities of the fifty-nine institutions in the North Carolina Community College System. Among this and many other distinctions, your school can also claim the president of the North Carolina Community College System, former Congressman Martin Lancaster, a native of Wayne County and the husband of a former WCC history instructor, Alice Lancaster. He chose your campus as the site of his installation ceremony.

Fall Semester 2000 saw 3,001 students like you enrolled ast Wayne Community College in the more than fifty curriculum programs offered. Spring Semester 2001 enrollment was 3,040. Many students took advantage of online courses, telecourses, distance learning, and weekend programs as well as the additional WCC course offerings at Seymour Johnson Air Force Base. As the introduction reminds you, this college exists for YOU. It offers numerous diploma programs and associate degree programs. It also provides an adult basic education program, a continuing education occupational program, and a community services program.

The purpose of the college is to serve individuals, business and industry, and other groups in the service area with quality, economical, convenient learning opportunities to meet student and community needs. Six specific purposes focus directly or indirectly on YOU. Of the long-range goals designed to fulfill the purpose of WCC, the very first was written with you in mind: "STUDENTS—Provide educational and support programs that reduce factors inhibiting student success." In fact, all seven goals involving educational programs, faculty and staff, administration and finance, facilities, institutional development, and community indicate a desire to serve you and your needs.

Finding Your Way Around Campus

Look on the ground at prominent corners of the buildings. Brown signs display names of buildings in white print.

Wayne Learning Center Building

The first and most obvious building, easily visible from Highway 70 Bypass and many other surrounding points, the big octagonal one with the flags out front, is the main building. Named after the Library or Learning Center on its third floor, this

WAYNE COMMUNITY COLLEGE

3000 Wayne Memorial Drive
PO Box 8002
Goldsboro, NC 27530-8002

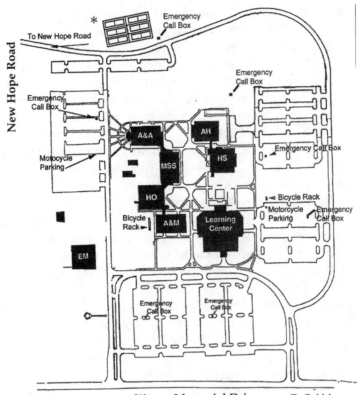

Legend of Buildings

A&A - Magnolia -Agriculture and Automotive Building
AH - Pine -Allied Health Building
A&M - Dogwood -Arts and Mathematics Building
EM - Cedar - Energy & Maintenance Building
HO - Hocutt Building
HS - Holly -Health Science Building
LC - Wayne Learning Center
MSS - Azalea -Mechanical and Social Science Building
* - Elmer H. Crumpler Tennis Complex

building houses administration and many facilities vital to you and your college career. As you enter the front doors of LC, you see the switchboard where all incoming phone calls are received. Directly behind the switchboard is the office of Security. Lost and Found is located there.

To the right of the switchboard is the Business and Industry/Small Business Center. To the left is the hallway leading to an area you visited when you came to WCC for admission, counseling, and placement testing: Student Development. The first left off that hallway is the Information Systems office where all computer and telephone operations are coordinated. Admissions and Records is a few yards ahead on your right, followed on your left and straight ahead by counselors' offices in the front corner. At your second right turn, you are at the registration window where you can inquire about schedules, grade reports, transcripts, and other records.

Turning from that window, you are in the Financial Aid area. Double doors on both sides of Financial Aid lead into the Atrium. One set opens almost directly on the Cashier's window where you will pay your tuition, pick up Pell Grant checks, or use an automatic teller machine.

The Atrium is the bright center of first floor LC. Heading back toward the front of the building, you will pass administrative offices including those of the president and two vice presidents. Don't go back out the front door, however; much of your life on campus will involve the back side of LC and the second and third floors as well as the other buildings on campus.

The back half of first floor LC includes the Bookstore located near the entrance on the south side of the building (that's the side nearer the hospital and Highway 70). The cafeteria is in that southeast corner. The middle of the back half of LC is the Lecture Hall where you will likely spend many hours for entertainment and information while you are a student at WCC.

The back north corner of first floor LC is literally your corner: it houses the Student Lounge complete with pool tables, ping pong tables, video games, and a patio for eating and socializing as well as the Student Activities Office where you can have your student ID card made, pick up a Y pass, or get an appointment for medical services on Wednesdays. Circling back past Student Activities toward the front of LC, you will see elevators and the more obvious stairway approximately in the center of the Atrium.

On second floor LC are the offices of instructors in accounting, administrative office technology, business administration, business computer programming, and fashion merchandising and marketing. Classrooms for those programs as well as for other classes such as English and math are located on the circular second floor. Elevator, external stairs on the north side, and the atrium stairway all lead to third floor.

Third floor LC may well become your home away from home, for it is the site of the library. The circular facility overlooks the atrium and has study areas on its balcony, a favorite spot for study groups. The library is open from 7:45 A.M. until 9:00 P.M. Monday through Thursday and until 5:00 P.M. Friday; Saturday hours of 10:00 until 2:00 are offered on most weekends when school is in session. Your class will tour the library, and you may get a specialized tour in some other classes such as English 113. (Read more about the library in Chapter 7.)

One of the most common tips for new students from students and faculty alike is to become familiar with your college library, so begin to investigate it on your own as soon as possible. Even before you need to consult its resources, consider finding your own favorite spot for study: the balcony, a carrel, a table near the stacks.

On the rear exterior side of third floor LC opening off the library is another area that may become exceedingly important to you while you are at WCC: Academic Skills Center. This facility provides academic support services including individualized instruction, tutoring, and materials to help you with courses in reading, English, math, science, business, computer, and others. ASC maintains the same hours as the library, and computerized log-in is a simple matter.

On the front exterior side of third floor LC is the media production center with its own darkroom and studio. The print shop is on the north corner between elevator and outside stairs. Near the circulation desk is one last set of stairs leading to a mezzanine with another facility where you can find help with your courses: the Writing Center. At the Writing Center you can make an appointment with an English instructor who will help you organize, proofread, edit, and revise your papers; you may also use the computers to do your word processing. (Read more about academic assistance in Chapter 11.)

As you see, LC Building may become one of your major destinations on this campus. Large entrances on four sides make it accessible from all parking areas and from all other buildings. Behind it is a patio where many students eat and socialize, and beyond that patio are a simple amphitheater (some students call it the pit or the swimming pool without water, and you may find aerobics classes there or drama students doing improvisation there) and a focal point of the center of campus: the Spillway. This metal structure created by sculptor Jim Galucci was given to the college by Goldsboro Milling Company in honor of its long-time employee Billy Shepard. Students often describe the sculpture for a writing assignment and even more often watch for its periodic dumping of water into the fountain. (The back cover of this book features the Spillway.)

Holly Building

Directly behind LC is a building smaller than LC but similar in design. Formerly known as HS for Health and Science, its name is Holly. On the first floor is the dental program. The dental clinic offers students many dental services for a small fee and occasionally for free! When dental students need patients in order to complete their graduation requirements, the Dental Department advertises its services such as teeth cleaning on CAMNET. The elevator is outside next to the rear stairway. Second floor has offices of biology, chemistry, and physics instructors as well as classrooms and labs for the sciences. You may occasionally have a class other than science scheduled in Holly.

Pine Building

A breezeway at both levels of Holly Building leads to Pine, formerly called the Allied Health Building. Its first floor is the home of Basic Skills, Human Resources Development, the Literacy Center, and the Basic Skills Computer Lab. Second floor houses the Nursing Department and the Medical Assisting Department.

Tennis Courts and Ball Field

Behind Pine Building is an area used for physical education classes, intramural sports, and events like Spring Fling. Located here are a fenced ball field and new-in-1997 hard surfaced tennis courts named for their donor, Elmer Crumpler of Pikeville. Students, faculty, and staff have first choice of tennis courts any time they are not in use for classes or for scheduled matches or tournaments.

The beautiful wooded landscape across the back side of campus is more than just a scenic spot; it includes plantings of use to students in forestry and other agricultural and natural resources programs. The greenhouses in that area are the home of the Continuing Education horticulture program.

Magnolia Building

Walkways lead from Holly and Pine Buildings to a complex of four buildings on the north side of campus. The rear one is the newest on the north side; classes moved into Magnolia in late 1996. On first floor is the Automotive Lab as well as the Air Conditioning, Heating and Refrigeration Lab. Upstairs are numerous classrooms, agriculture labs, and the Open Computer Lab (215) which has generous hours to accommodate students' needs. Find 215 soon! More than fifty computers have Internet, e-mail accounts, and software used in most courses.

Azalea Building

A curving breezeway connects Magnolia to Azalea, the home of Mechanical and Social Sciences. Its first floor houses the Machine Shop and Auto Body Shop with classrooms and offices. An elevator opens just inside the rear entrance, and stairway entrances are on the right from front doors and on the right from the rear doors of first floor. Second floor has large classrooms used for criminal justice, law enforcement, psychology, sociology, history, health, and other classes. A weight room (207) and locker rooms provide a fitness center for physical education classes as well as for individual use by students, faculty, and staff. Second floor opens on its west end to a breezeway connecting Azalea with Hocutt and Dogwood Buildings.

Third floor has offices for faculty and staff in human services, early childhood, psychology, sociology, history, health and physical education, criminal justice, law enforcement, agricultural sciences, forestry, park ranger technology, and automotive.

Hocutt Building

Hocutt Building, referred to as "HO" on course schedules and maps of campus, was the first classroom building on this campus and is the only building named for a person. The 1976 groundbreaking ceremony initiated many years of a single classroom building finally surrounded by all the others you now use. Hocutt's first floor has a large welding shop and the ASEP area which connects Wayne Community College with General Motors Corporation. Second floor has classrooms and offices of instructors in drafting, transportation, mechanical studies, and engineering programs. Aviation instructors have offices here as well as on their own campus, the airport. (You may have other types of classes scheduled in Hocutt as well.)

Dogwood Building

The final building connected to the breezeway is Dogwood, formerly called Arts and Mathematics, beside the main building on the front north corner of campus. First floor has several facilities you will want to investigate. The area nearer LC includes Planning and Research, the Foundation (source of thousands of dollars in scholarships), Public Information, Co-op, and Job Referral. (Chapter 11 will tell you more about Co-op and Job Referral.) The other side of first floor has the offices of Continuing Education and Workforce Preparedness.

In the middle across the front is the area where you took placement tests, 145A & 145 B. The horizontal first floor hallway near the back has three large classrooms with partitions that open to provide space for large gatherings, 124–126. Across the hall in 120 is the Career Assessment and Training Center, a place you definitely need to visit. (See Chapter 11.) An elevator and two stairways lead to second and third floors.

Second floor contains classrooms most often used for math and liberal arts (English, art, music, drama, speech, reading, journalism, humanities, foreign languages, and religion.) Dogwood 206 is the big, bright art classroom, and 201 is a large music room surrounded by special practice rooms. On third floor are the offices of your liberal arts and math instructors.

North Entrance and New Hope Road Entrance

At the north entrance to campus, you will see the beginnings of a golf green for students in the Turfgrass Management Technology program. The tall eagle-topped structure near the entrance is a war memorial to American soldiers who gave their lives serving their country. Next is the maintenance complex, one of the two oldest structures on campus. The New Hope Road entrance opened in 1999, providing another approach to campus.

Parking

On all four sides of these buildings are parking areas. As on all college campuses, parking is very competitive, but all undesignated spaces are reserved for students. Plan ahead for a possible traffic jam on Wayne Memorial Drive on the first days of class, especially in the fall, and consider using the north entrance or the rear entrance as an alternative to the traffic light entrance early in the morning and again around 1:00 when many students finish classes and leave for work. New parking areas and the New Hope Road rear entrance opened in May 1999.

Ask for a Tour!

Remind your academic advisor and your ACA 111 instructor that you need a tour during your early days at WCC. Not knowing your way around is a common ailment easily cured! Take a few minutes for a self-guided tour as well, and notice the various facilities near your classrooms. If you encounter necessary places not mentioned in these pages, please mention them to your ACA 111 instructor to help future students find their way around. You will become the expert on what students really need to know; share your expertise with others.

Well, here you are on a beautiful campus. It's all yours! What will you do with it? "Quality You Can See" at Wayne Community College means much more than a beautiful campus. YOU ARE HERE. What next?

(Thanks to Leasa Holmes, Linwood Anderson, and Grace Lutz)

Chapter Three

Textbooks and Other Publications You Need

Books! The library is filled with them (more than 42,000 at last count). Your instructors' offices are filled with them. (A student entered one WCC instructor's office and exclaimed, "Whoa! Look at all these words!") Books are part of a meaningful life. Thoreau advises, "Read the best books first, or you may not have a chance to read them at all," and according to Cicero, "A room without books is like a body without a soul."

Textbooks

Textbooks, heavy and expensive, will be a big part of your life as a college student. The College Bookstore is on the first floor of LC Building just outside the cafeteria. Regular hours at the Bookstore are as follows:

Monday–Friday	8:30 A.M.–4:00 P.M.
Tuesday and Wednesday	6:30 P.M.–8:30 P.M.

Special hours are as follows:

First day of classes each semester   8:30 A.M.–8:30 P.M.
First two weeks of classes   Extra Monday and Thursday hours 6:30–8:30 P.M.
First two Saturdays of each semester   9:00 A.M.–12:00 noon

Special book sales at Seymour Johnson Air Force Base Education Center:

First two days of classes on base each term   9:00 A.M.–4:30 P.M.

The bookstore also sells course supplies, novelties, greeting cards, school shirts and other clothing with WCC emblem, and graduation items (caps and gowns, invitations.)

Most instructors do not expect you to buy your books until you have met classes the first day; however, some departments do post a list of required texts. Pell Grant students need to purchase all of their books and supplies at one time. However, under special circumstances, Financial Aid can provide a second voucher. If a course is cancelled, you may return your book provided you have not written in it.

You will sometimes be able to buy used texts from other students or from the Used Bookstore operated in the cafeteria the last two exam days of each semester. Be careful, though, that the edition you purchase is indeed the one to be used in your class. Some of your texts you will prefer not to sell but to keep as a part of your own personal or professional library. The handbook assigned for your English composition class, for example, is a "keeper" as a ready reference for grammar, punctuation, documentation, and business use such as letter and resume writing.

CAMNET

Television monitors in all buildings broadcast announcements of activities, scholarships, important academic and financial deadlines, and other news. **Read CAMNET daily** to stay informed.

The *Student Handbook*

Your *Student Handbook* is available free in the Student Activities office. It contains a calendar crucial to your schedule. Dates of registration, preregistration, midterm, last day to drop classes, exams, and student activities appear on this calendar. The handbook also contains *vital* details on every topic from the attendance policy to the withdrawal procedure, from where to have your ID card made to how to calculate your grade point average, from SGA bylaws to student clubs and honors. It contains rules you must follow. For example, a new policy requires cell phones, beepers, and walkie-talkies to be in quiet position in class, in labs, and in the library. Being aware of policies is <u>YOUR</u> responsibility. Read every word in the *Handbook*.

WCC General Catalog

You need a college catalog if you do not already have one! The Office of Admissions and Records maintains a supply. The catalog contains important information about admissions, expenses, financial aid; the college's operating dates; data on faculty and staff; campus maps; student life and academic regulations; course descriptions; and every program available at WCC. The most important pages of all will vary from student to student, for they contain the description of each program and the course requirements for that program. Your individual graduation requirements appear in the catalog current at the time of your initial continuous enrollment in your program at WCC. You should clip or rubber band or in some way mark the page where *your* curriculum requirements appear! You share with your academic advisor the responsibility for monitoring your progress toward your degree.

The "Tabloid"

About a week before phone registration and preregistration, the college publishes its schedule of courses for the next semester in small newspaper format. Use this schedule to prepare for your conference with your advisor when you will plan your next semester's course load.

Notice the evening courses always printed in a gray block near the front of the tabloid and the Seymour Johnson Air Force Base courses in a special block inside the tabloid. Also notice the exam schedule; most instructors announce the exam date early in the course, but you can identify your own exam schedule as soon as you have registered for your classes by matching the time of each class with the exam time designated for that class hour.

(Naturally students are excited and curious when the tabloid comes out; they want to know who's teaching what when! Nevertheless, resist the temptation to study the tabloid in class; you cannot take next semester's classes until you have completed your current ones! Most instructors will be happier if you study the tabloid on your own time!)

The *Campus Voice*

The WCC Campus Voice is a product of the journalism classes. JOU 111 is a three-hour humanities elective offered under English instructor Liz Meador. Students who wish to pursue the course beyond the first semester may register for a two-hour weekly section for one hour of credit. Being a member of the *Voice* staff/journalism class allows students to experience interviewing, taking photos, writing copy, laying out copy, and selling ads to produce a twenty-plus-page newspaper that highlights campus events. Copies of the paper are free through your student activities fee.

Renaissance

Another publication for and by students is *Renaissance,* the artists' and writers' magazine. The May 2001 issue was the seventeenth annual edition. Students produce more than ninety-five percent of the art work, poetry, essays, and short stories published in *Renaissance.* Faculty and staff contribute the remainder. If you wish to submit some of your own work for consideration, see one of the editors (Rosalyn Lomax, Kathryn Spicer, Paula Sauls) or anyone in Liberal Arts, Dogwood 3rd Floor. Cash awards go to students for the outstanding essay, poetry, short story, art, and cover design.

Admissions and Registration Information

The booklet of information that contained your application to Wayne Community College is an important source of details brought together from your catalog and other publications. Review it carefully! Also read and keep the materials mailed to you before preregistration each semester.

Competency Statements, Course Handouts, Syllabi

Consider any handouts your instructors give you as additions to your textbooks. Course competency statements identify the concepts and activities you can expect to encounter in each course. These statements reflect the belief of the North Carolina Community College System that every course you take should make you competent in the principles of that course and their application. You may use these statements to keep track of material to be covered as well as your grades on the assessments of required tasks.

You may also receive a handout providing specific requirements of the course as well as departmental policies. The handout may include or accompany a syllabus detailing your assignments, test dates, and paper or project dates. Instructors will expect you to be responsible for meeting deadlines and fulfilling requirements listed on the syllabus, perhaps without additional reminders.

EXERCISES USING YOUR ESSENTIAL PUBLICATIONS

1. Using the calendar in your *Student Handbook,* find the following dates for the current semester:

    Midterm _____

    Last Day to Drop _____

    Last Day of Classes _____

    TRY (Telephone Preregistration) _____
    (If not on calendar, dates will appear on CAMNET.)

    Preregistration _____

    "The doctor is in"—Make arrangements for a free appointment at Healthwise by going to Student Activities

    on _____day_ by _____A.M.

2. Using your catalog, list your program requirements below.

    _____

    _____

    _____

    _____

    _____

3. Using your *Student Handbook*, identify the following:

President of WCC _____

Vice President, Academic Affairs and Student Services _____

Vice President, Educational Support Services _____

Vice President, Continuing Education _____

Student Activities Coordinator _____

SGA President _____

SGA Vice President _____

SGA Secretary _____

Other SGA Officers _____

4. Using the exam schedule in the tabloid (or a copy provided by your instructor), figure out your own exam schedule for this semester.

Course	Exam Date	Exam Hours
_____	_____	_____
_____	_____	_____
_____	_____	_____
_____	_____	_____
_____	_____	_____

Feeling Good about Yourself and Your Future

Someone you need to know well is *yourself!* Spend some time with yourself! Answer these questions about yourself.

What are three of my positive qualities?

_____

_____

_____

What have I done lately that made me proud?

_____

_____

If you pondered even a moment before answering those questions, you may not be giving yourself all the credit you deserve. YOU ARE SPECIAL. Do you remember the movie *Steel Magnolias*? When M'Lynn (Sally Field) says to her daughter Shelby (Julia Roberts) through clenched teeth, "You are special!" she is concerned that her diabetic daughter's desire for a baby has blinded her to the dangers involved in pregnancy of a diabetic woman. Those words apply to *you* as well as to Shelby, but for different reasons.

Starting a college career is a big step for anyone—for students just out of high school, for students who have waited a few years between high school and college, for students whose college education was interrupted earlier and who are starting over now, for students who are still in high school but are taking some college classes through dual enrollment or JumpStart—coming to college is a big step. One of many special things about you is that *you are in college.*

Non-traditional students, sometimes defined as those not between eighteen and twenty-two, often feel especially insecure when they enter college. Many older students, those over forty or thirty or even twenty-five, confess that they expected to be the oldest one in every class. Surprise! Often they are not in the minority at all. Non-traditional students bring with them some qualities and experiences and abilities that will greatly enhance their lives as college students. Even though they feel out of practice, their special factors give them the same degree of edge (although a different kind) as traditional students still in practice from their more recent high school days.

Poets and philosophers have written many words about how special each human being is and thus about how special you are. In his essay "Self-Reliance," Ralph Waldo Emerson advises, "Trust thyself." His contemporary Thoreau reminds us to choose our own paths in life, to dare to be ourselves; he desires each person to "be very careful to find out and pursue *his own* way, and not his father's or his mother's or his neighbor's instead."

A wise professor at Marymount College, John Lawry, has published the letters he wrote to his daughter when she was in college. In one letter he speaks to her about being herself:

> It is not always easy to be ourselves. The first step is really to hear what is going on with us. The masks we wear for the benefit of others often deceive us as well. It is important that we learn to be ourselves. We do this by stopping the attempt to be somebody else. (29)

He continues, "You must be yourself. If you want to change or grow, you have to accept where you are and be who you are"(Lawry 29).

A senior at Boston College reflects on his experiences as a first-year student at two different colleges: "The greatest challenge I had faced was the challenge of being me"(Hartman ix). Even as you grow, as you develop yourself, as you enhance yourself, never lose sight of who you really are. Be yourself!

According to a very practical textbook called *Student Success,* your success in life is controlled by "your self-esteem, self-confidence, self-concept, and self-image," and developing "a strong 'self' depends on how you want to think about yourself and how you want to behave, and it is totally under your control" (Walter and

Siebert 32). College offers you unlimited opportunities to develop the strong self that accepts responsibility for the consequences of your actions. *The Road Less Traveled* asserts, "The feeling of being valuable—'I am a valuable person'—is essential to mental health and is a cornerstone of self-discipline" (Peck 24). College offers you unlimited opportunities to show yourself and the world how valuable you are and what you can do. Believe you are valuable.

Jimmie Ford, now retired, was a vice president who often spoke to ACA 111 classes. Mr. Ford has generously agreed to let his advice be shared in this chapter. Like Benjamin Franklin in *The Way to Wealth,* he has gleaned his wisdom from his experiences and those of others. One of his most memorable challenges to students involves accepting themselves as they are and working from there. He tells students to go home, strip, gaze at themselves in the mirror nightly for two weeks; at the end of that time, if they still see the same image each night, then they should conclude, "Hey, this is it! This is what I have been given to work with, so I might as well get used to it and make the best of it." If you do want to make a change that is possible, you must be willing to take a risk in order to implement that change.

TAKE A RISK? One of the saddest characters in the 1963 play *Spoon River Anthology* is George Gray. (Incidentally, if you take sociology, you will probably have Ray Brannon, the instructor who played George Gray in the WCC production of this play.) Gray realizes after his death that the boat carved on his tombstone represents the way he lived his life, never really leaving the harbor because he was unwilling to take a risk. How sad to look back on a life full of fear and devoid of meaning.

Ambition, goals, education, life—these are calling you! You have answered by coming to college. Listen for the next call. Do not hide or shrink from your goals: YOU CAN DO IT.

A familiar Christian pledge involves using what we have: "I will do the best I can with what I have and what I am. . . ." That pledge applies to success in college as well as to spiritual matters. Use what you have and what you are today to do the best you can. With that attitude toward college, you will find opportunities to do your best and to make your best better.

On a list of "Twenty-one Ways to Succeed in College," professors at the University of South Carolina include the following: "Learn to appreciate yourself more. Hey, you got this far!" (Jewler, Gardner, and Owens 9). One WCC student submitted this same advice on a list of tips for you.

Here at WCC you will find many supportive faculty, staff, and students surrounding you and encouraging you. You may also have friends and family who provide positive reinforcement for your college efforts. If, however, you encounter negative voices that threaten to dampen your spirits or hinder your progress, be strong and be swift to silence those voices. As Jimmie Ford advises, if you find people around you bringing you down, shake them loose! English instructor Kathryn Spicer says she decided a few years ago to try not to be around anybody who does not make her feel good about herself. Following that advice may not always be possible (you may not be able to quit your job or move out to escape negative acquaintances), but when you have a choice, pick upbeat, helpful, positive companions. When you do not have a choice, remind yourself constantly that you are special. Don't ever let yourself forget that. Eleanor Roosevelt believed that no one can make you feel inferior without your permission.

In this class you may have an opportunity to take a personality profile that will help you understand co-workers, friends, or family members with whom you have conflicts. The Career Center counselor in A&M 120 can tell you all about this opportunity. Go make an appointment!

In your college classes, if you ever encounter students who exhibit what you consider a "superior" attitude, give yourself a chance to get to know them. You may be surprised to learn that they actually feel just as insecure as you have let them make you feel! You may even become friends.

Many people are here to help you succeed and be your best self, but ultimately, you are responsible for making this happen. Learning, growing, getting a college education, getting a life, becoming a happy and successful person—these can happen *for* you, but they won't happen *without* you.

Walt Whitman's voice in "Song of Myself" promises a guide:

> My left hand hooking you round the waist,
> My right hand pointing to landscapes of continents
> and the public road.
> Not I, not any one else can travel that road for
> you,
> You must travel it for yourself.

You can take that road. No one else can do it for you, but you are quite capable of doing it yourself. Along the way at WCC are many people willing to help point you in the right direction, to guide you, to cheer for you, but you must walk that road for yourself. Sir Winston Churchill reportedly delivered a commencement address with only three main words, "Never give up." You can do whatever you set out to do; you can be whatever you set out to be. Don't wait. Seize the day. Just do it! (No Nikes required—just do it.)

(Thanks to Jimmie Ford, Terrell Roberts, Manuel Dudley, and the counselors for their many presentations in ACA 111 classes)

SPEND A LITTLE TIME WITH YOURSELF.

Write a few sentences about a time when you were afraid to attempt something.

_____

_____

_____

Name one college challenge that you fear.

_____

_____

_____

What could be the worst possible outcome if you accept that challenge?

_____

_____

_____

What could be the best possible outcome if you accept it?

_____

_____

_____

Write three positive statements about yourself.

1._____

2._____

3._____

Reminder: Recognizing your strong points is not the same as being conceited.

Develop your own personal motto reminding yourself that *you are unique* and *you can do great things.* Tape it on your steering wheel or bathroom mirror.

_____

_____

_____

_____

_____

Chapter Five

Time for Time Management

COLLEGE is *not* a four-letter word. However, quite a few four-letter words do affect your performance in college. One of them is the topic of the previous chapter: *self*. Another is *work* and how much of that you are willing to exert. Perhaps another of those most important four-letter words for college and for life is *time*.

Fill in the blanks with whatever you have heard yourself say in the past week:

"I don't have time to ___do extra cleaning___."

"I'll never get around to ___cleaning the utility shed___

"I wish I had time to ___take more bible class___."

"I'll never finish ___this paper___ in time."

If you have not made one or more of those statements in desperation or frustration recently, you must be quite unusual. Most human beings suffer from the condition described by Andrew Marvell in the seventeenth century: "But at my back I always hear / Time's winged chariot hurrying near." (Marvell, of course, is using the *carpe diem* rationale for his speaker's arguments to rush his lady into a relationship in "To His Coy Mistress," a typical seventeenth century love poem.) Poets have always portrayed time with wings. John Milton, another seventeenth century poet, bewails the quick arrival of his twenty-fourth birthday: "How soon hath Time, that subtle thief of youth, / Stol'n on his wing my three and twentieth year." The first American poet ever published, Anne Bradstreet, speaks of how we waste our time, shortening even further our already short lives "in eating, drinking, sleeping, vain delight." Benjamin Franklin warns: "Dost thou love life, then do not squander time, for that's the stuff life is made of."

If these writers can put you on a guilt trip for the amount of time you spend sleeping or watching tv or chilling, perhaps you could use a bit of Henry David Thoreau's philosophy; Thoreau worries that we place too much emphasis on rushing and succeeding and getting ready for life at the cost of life itself. He says he went to Walden Pond to live slowly and deliberately so that he would not come to the end of life and discover that he had not yet lived. His *Walden* should encourage students who take their time getting through college (and those whose multiple roles force them to take longer than the traditional four years to finish):

> Why should we be in such desperate haste to succeed? If a man does not keep pace with his companions, perhaps it is because he hears a different drummer. Let him step to the music which he hears, however measured or far away. Shall he turn his spring into summer?

Long before any of these writers expressed their concerns about time, the wisdom of the Bible had already addressed our four-letter word:

> To everything there is a season, and a time to every purpose under the heaven:
>   A time to be born, and a time to die;
>   a time to plant, and a time to pluck up that which is planted;
>   A time to kill, and a time to heal;
>   a time to break down, and a time to build up;
>   A time to weep, and a time to laugh;
>   a time to mourn, and a time to dance;
>   A time to cast away stones, and a time to gather stones together;
>   a time to embrace, and a time to refrain from embracing;
>   A time to get, and a time to lose;
>   a time to keep, and a time to cast away;
>   A time to rend, and a time to sew;
>   a time to keep silence, and a time to speak;
>   A time to love, and a time to hate;
>   a time of war, and a time of peace.

> (Ecclesiastes 3.1–8)

Time! How often do you look at your watch? At the clock in the classroom or your workplace? How do you fill your hours? Do you manage your time, or does time manage you? A college staff member who has spoken to many ACA 111 classes is Bill Thompson, Director of Planning and Research. He agrees with other time management specialists that time management is one way of giving ourselves some control over our lives.

A Few Tips

1. Use a daily planning guide and a calendar. Memory is simply not adequate to keep track of all assignments and deadlines. Consolidate your syllabi into a personal calendar. Create a process/steps calendar for assignments. Start at the end of your semester calendar and work backwards when planning your to-do-list.

2. Prioritize your assignments/chores/activities. Most experts prescribe an A, B, C approach.
   A: things that *must* be done immediately.
   B: things that you would be working on if you did not have the A items; work on these next.
   C: things that can wait until A and B items are done (and possibly forever).

3. Not only will you be at Wayne Community College a relatively short time; each semester lasts only sixteen weeks, and your individual classes last only 48± hours. GO TO CLASS! Get the most out of those few hours allotted to each course.

4. Use tiny blocks of time effectively. *Waiting* time too often becomes *wasted* time. Carry index cards with small study details; pull them out while you are waiting in line somewhere or waiting for a doctor or a haircutter.
   Carry a note pad and use waiting time to make a list of the night's commitments or the next day's commitments or even a grocery list.

5. Make reasonable to-do lists, not impossible ones.

6. Finally, think of *time* another way: what is your *best* time of day? Theories about biological clocks, biorhythms, and other approaches to what you may simply call your best time of day deserve your acknowledgment. Schedule your most difficult classes during your best time if possible. Plan your study sessions during your best time if possible. If you know you will surely fall asleep during an afternoon study session, perhaps you should schedule a nap or physical activity at that time and save your study session for a time when you are most wide awake (although Thoreau says he never met anyone who was truly awake).

Although the Declaration of Independence reminds us that all people are created equal, not all students have identical resources. Financial, intellectual, and personal resources vary from one student to another. Even the resource of time available for college varies from one student to another, but the number of hours in a day does not vary; everybody gets 24. What you have to do in a day's time may be more or less than what the student sitting beside you has to do, but both of you have the same number of hours each day to do whatever it is that you have to do. How do you spend your time? Accounting for every hour may surprise you. Take a few minutes to examine your time and how you spend the 168 hours granted to you each week. Fill in the chart on page 37.

Look at your time chart. The way you spend your time involves two categories of time use: first, the activities that you *must* do (like sleep and eat) and those you *must* do at a certain time like work or class; and second, the activities that you can juggle or rearrange. *Fixed* and *flexible* are good labels for these two kinds of time commitments. List your activities accordingly:

FIXED   *FLEXIBLE*

_____   _____

_____   _____

_____   _____

_____   _____

_____   _____

_____   _____

Have you included time for family and time for friends? How about some time for yourself? Think back to the four-letter word *self*. Success in college and in life requires you to take care of yourself both physically and emotionally, so don't forget time to keep yourself healthy. Mr. Thompson always encourages students to put on both lists some activity that allows them to relax or take care of themselves; his is another four-letter word: *fish*. What is yours?

The way you manage your time has much to do with how you view your commitments.

1. Are you a procrastinator? _____

2. Are you a perfectionist? _____

3. Are you good at telling other people you are busy? _____

4. Are your goals clear to you? _____

Your answers play an important role in how well you manage your time. Consider your responses.

1. *Are* you a procrastinator? Being a procrastinator is not a crime; it is not even a terrible character flaw, but it can certainly make your life miserable! Most procrastinators rationalize that they work better under pressure, and a little pressure may indeed make your creative juices and your adrenaline flow. (Nothing like a deadline to set those fingers to the keyboard! John Steinbeck's *Working Days*, his journal of the writing of *The Grapes of Wrath*, often mentions his daily goal of what he felt he *must* complete, whether a certain chapter or characterization or plot detail.) However, consistent procrastination can be a major source of stress. Overcoming or coping with a tendency to procrastinate may well be your key to effective time management and to good study habits, two essential elements in college success. Breaking a big project down into small steps may help you prevent procrastination on your assignments. If you are a procrastinator, think about the class that will demand the greatest attention to keeping up this semester. Write a pledge or reminder about that class in the following space:

_____

_____

_____

_____

_____

2. Next, are you a perfectionist? "Yes" is not necessarily the best answer to this one. If you are determined to perfect each step of a project before moving on to the next step, you may never finish! Some good advice for you may be to get the job *done* first and then go back and perfect each part.

3. How good are you at managing the way other people use your time? If you feel you owe other people as much of your time as they want, you may not have any time left for school! Learn to say *no*!

Family responsibilities are a priority, but you will need to set some rules and have an understanding with family members about the uninterrupted time you must devote to studies. You also must discipline yourself to be honest with friends who drop by or telephone while you are studying. (Someone should write a poem about the notorious time stealer, the phone! How much time have you spent on the phone in the past week?) How much time does your family require in order for you to feel that you are being fair to them and fulfilling your commitment to them?

4. Finally, do you have a clear picture of your academic and personal goals? *Goal* is another of those all-important four-letter words. Knowing where you want to go is crucial to getting there. Make periodic check-ups to see how you are progressing and to see how your goals have changed.

List some of your short-range and long-range goals.

NEXT WEEK

_____

_____

_____

NEXT MONTH

_____

_____

_____

NEXT YEAR

_____

_____

_____

FIVE YEARS FROM NOW

_____

_____

_____

TEN YEARS FROM NOW

_____

_____

_____

How interesting that we use the same verb with *money* that we use with *time* and with *life*: *spend*. Author Annie Dillard reminds us that the way we spend our days is really the way we spend our lives. How we use or pass our time is how we use or pass our lives. Thus managing our time is managing our lives.

How many people spend their lives waiting to be happy or to feel successful or to start really living when some certain moment arrives or when some certain event takes place? A writing called "The Station" by Robert J. Hastings reminds us not to spend our lives *waiting* to enjoy something but to enjoy the time as it passes. Jay Martin, a Presbyterian minister, speaks of the "when . . . then . . ." club. Too many people say, "When I finish college, then I'll be happy," or "When I make my first million, then I'll be really successful," or "When I retire, then I'll enjoy life." Don't wait till *then*. Make the most of *now*. (The *carpe diem* philosophy remains appropriate.)

TIME: one of your most valuable resources in college and in life—manage it at least as carefully as you do your money and perhaps more carefully, for you can get more money, but when your time is up, you can't get any more time!

525,600—do you recognize that figure? Suppose it were your annual salary dollars! Actually it represents something far more valuable: the number of minutes in a year. Suppose someone gave you that much money to spend as you wish and not pay back just as long as you could account for every penny of it. Well, you have been given the time.

Carpe diem!

HURRY UP PLEASE IT'S TIME!

(T.S. Eliot)

(Special thanks to Bill Thompson for sharing time management ideas and for his numerous presentations in ACA 111 classes)

Name _____

Date _____

"The Week That Was"
Your Current Time Schedule

	Monday	Tuesday	Wednesday	Thursday	Friday	Saturday	Sunday
6:00 A.M.							
7:00 A.M.							
8:00 A.M.							
9:00 A.M.							
10:00 A.M.							
11:00 A.M.							
noon							
1:00 P.M.							
2:00 P.M.							
3:00 P.M.							
4:00 P.M.							
5:00 P.M.							
6:00 P.M.							
7:00 P.M.							
8:00 P.M.							
9:00 P.M.							
10:00 P.M.							
11:00 P.M.							
midnight							
1:00 A.M.							
2:00 A.M.							

Totals:

Hours Spent in Class   ___   168   (total hours in 1 week)

Hours Spent Studying   ___   –___   (your total of "necessary hours")

Hours Spent Sleeping   ___   (hours unaccounted for weekly)

Hours Spent Eating   ___

Hours Spent Working   ___   7⌐   (hours unaccounted for PER DAY!)

                 Total   ___

Divide the total weekly hours unaccounted for by 7 to learn how many daily hours you cannot account for! How *are* you using those hours?

Reconsider! Did you fill a one-hour slot with a twenty-minute activity? How do you use the remaining minutes?

Chapter Six

Study Skills:
Making Your
Study Time Count

NOTE: If you are taking the Study Skills course, some of the material in this chapter will be very familiar to you. Please share the best information you have learned in Study Skills with your ACA 111 classmates and instructor.

People who really love knowledge never stop studying and learning. For you as a college student, studying is not an option but a requirement. Perhaps the bottom line is that you should study whether you have any specific homework or not. In fact, what may surprise many new college students is that some college instructors do not make daily assignments; they assume that you have the maturity to handle long-term assignments without reminders. They also assume that you are responsible for following the syllabus and other handouts and knowing deadlines and test dates without reminders. They definitely intend for you to regard reading assignments with the same urgency as written work requirements. When no specific assignment is due the next day, you can be reading ahead, reviewing notes or problems from the previous class hour, working on the next project or paper, or studying for the next test. *Study something daily* (or nightly).

One college professor believes that what distinguishes the *A* student from all the others, even more than intelligence or motivation, is study skills; he also thinks that with good study skills, the average student in a typical course can make an *A* (Lawry 62). How would you grade your study skills and study habits as you enter college? Did you always give your best preparation and self-discipline to your classes in high school? If so, you are in a good position to continue and enhance your study life. If you did not, it is never too late; you can develop good study skills.

List some of your most effective study techniques below:

1. _____

2. _____

3. _____

Orientation classes like yours often work in small groups to generate a list of study tips. They usually suggest the following sound guidelines, perhaps including some of the same ones you listed above:

- Have a certain quiet place to study.

- Study regularly/daily. Review often. Don't procrastinate.

- Commit to a study schedule and stick to it.

- If possible, pick *your* best time, the time when you are most alert. (Even if you do not consider yourself a morning person, consider getting up an hour early to study when you are fresh; you may be surprised at how much more you can accomplish first thing in the morning rather than falling asleep at your desk or table over and over again late at night.)

- If possible, study when you are not already tired.

- Get organized. Assemble study materials before you start.

- Study in short blocks of time. Divide your study material or project into smaller sections or tasks.

- Use note cards for small bits of material.

- Use waiting time. (Those note cards are perfect while you wait for an appointment or even at a stop light!)

- Take notes. (Take notes on the lecture and on your reading assignments.)

- Make study questions as you work.

- Study alone. Study time should not be a social hour. (However, the next tip is also popular—and sound.)

- Form a study group or find a study partner. (Certain material lends itself to group study. Moreover, the different people in the group have different strong points; what one person has trouble with, another may understand perfectly.)

- Use tapes of lectures or notes to study while commuting.

- Know what you are responsible for learning.

- Get help as soon as you need it.

College offers much more freedom than high school, and with that freedom, much more responsibility for class attendance. *Going to class* is one of the most important study habits of all. A little math reveals exactly how much you are spending for each hour of class. (Don't forget to add to your basic tuition all your other expenses like books, transportation, child care if you have small children.) Cutting a class for frivolous reasons is like throwing money away.

You have read about the attendance policy at Wayne Community College, which reflects the philosophy that regular class attendance is essential. (Note: The attendance policy has recently been reviewed and may be changed by the time this third edition of your textbook is published.) You may receive class handouts that make perhaps the most significant point about absences: absence from class does not relieve you of the responsibility for what goes on in your absence. Most college instructors expect you to be informed and prepared when you arrive whether you were present last time or not. Be sure to have the phone number of one or more conscientious classmates so you can inquire about what you missed, and remember that all instructors have regular office hours, departmental staff who can take messages for them, and voice mail.

So you've come to class, you arrived on time, you're sitting near the front, you have your book and other supplies, and you've prepared your assignment. Wait! How well have you prepared that reading assignment? Even if you do not completely understand the material, having read the assignment familiarizes you with technical or other unfamiliar terms and proper names mentioned in the lecture. Before you go to class, be sure you have read your assignment.

Reading Tips

Getting your money's worth out of the hour and out of that expensive textbook requires some careful reading. Skimming the table of contents is a good start. How closely does it parallel your instructor's syllabus or handout? Before reading a chapter, preview it by noting its title, subheadings, illustrations, and any summary or questions at its end. Within the chapter, be an *active* reader. (The English 111 textbook emphasizes and models active reading.)

- Highlight your text. Using a highlighter is a fine idea as long as you do not find yourself highlighting everything! However, highlighting also means conversing with your text by underlining, starring, commenting in the margin. (Get your money's worth out of those margins; fill them with your responses to the material.)

- Note all boldfaced or italicized terms.
- Mark any unfamiliar terms.
- Have a dictionary for your companion! Use it to look up any words that you cannot figure out from the context.
- Stop frequently to ask yourself questions about what you have just read.
- Summarize main points aloud.
- Take notes outlining or summarizing.

Experts have developed many approaches to reading. SRSR prescribes surveying, reading, simplifying, and reflecting (Walther 48).

Dave Ellis (118–123) recommends "muscle reading": previewing; outlining; questioning; reading (every time your mind wanders, put a check mark on a scrap piece of paper, and don't try to read too long); underlining (Ellis says to enjoy marking in your books the way you were never allowed to as a child! Your marks leave signals for reviewing.); answering the questions you developed while previewing; reciting (talk out loud about what you have read); review within 24 hours; review regularly, perhaps weekly.

Other methods have in common with these two the steps of previewing or surveying the material; anticipating questions for yourself; reading; reciting aloud answers or summary of short passages; reviewing.

Perhaps your *reading* step would benefit from a few more basic reminders.

- Read your textbooks in a place conducive to concentration, as free of distractions as possible.
- Have good lighting. (The older you get, or the worse your vision gets, the more dependent you are on light for reading.)
- Be comfortable, but not too comfortable.
- Don't be physical: move only your eyes; avoid moving your lips or head; avoid vocalizing as you read. Any physical activity takes longer than the mental process of reading.
- Try to read in word groups rather than single words.

If you feel you need to improve your reading speed, comprehension, or vocabulary, consider taking Introduction to College Reading or Improved College Reading (RED 080 or 090) even if they are not requirements for you.

Back to Getting the Most Out of Class

You've read your assignment. Now let's try again. You're in class on time, up front, well supplied, and well prepared. What next? "Be here now" says it all. *Student Success: A Newsletter of College Survival* (January 1995) tells of two New Jersey instructors, Tracy Amerman and Susan Lancellotti, who advise their college students to SLANT for better attention and participation:

> **S**it up
>
> **L**ean forward
>
> **A**sk questions
>
> **N**od and smile
>
> **T**rack (follow the speaker with your eyes)

This process not only keeps you awake and alert; it also lets your instructor know you are really here! No speaker enjoys talking to a "glazed" group (or Krispy Kremes), as one WCC instructor calls a rather unresponsive morning class. Your instructors expect and appreciate respect, enthusiasm, interest, and energy. Most of them welcome appropriate interruptions for questions, comments, and discussions.

You may want to mention to your instructor any special circumstances such as working a night shift or having a sick child, not as an excuse but as a courtesy if you realize you may not be quite as alert as usual. Use your own judgment, depending on your relationship with the instructor and the nature of the class.

Taking Notes

Some instructors specify the kind of notebook or materials they prefer; others leave the choice up to you. However, all expect you to come to class equipped to take notes. Dating each class session's notes may help you find details or clarify an announcement later.

Taking notes does *not* mean trying to write down every word the instructor says. On the contrary, such an attempt makes it impossible for you to think and respond to lectures.

Most instructors follow some sort of plan or outline as they lecture, and their movement from one section to another or from one subtopic or example to another will probably be fairly obvious to you if you listen for transitional expressions and pauses; design your notes accordingly.

Any term or concept that your instructor repeats or writes on the board is worth noting. Remarks as obvious as "Remember this" or "This would be a great test question" may even be a part of your instructor's approach. Don't ignore those!

Develop your own system of abbreviations and symbols. It does not have to match anyone else's as long as *you* can decipher your own notes! You may incorporate math symbols like the three-dot triangle for "therefore"; shortcuts like "w/" for "with," use of consonants only like "btwn" for "between" since you hear the e sounds anyway, brief forms like "esp." for "especially"; foreign terms if shorter than the English counterpart; illustrations if you are a quick artist.

Whatever type of notebook you use, adapt it to the format of leaving blank space beside the page of notes. Taking class notes on only the front side of a spiral-bound or looseleaf page leaves the back of the preceding page free to use later for clarification, definitions, explanations, correlation with the textbook, questions for the instructor. The Cornell system of dividing the page with a vertical line into the right two-thirds for note-taking and the left third for later use has the same motive.

Taking notes in class is definitely a process that improves with practice and one that deserves your effort. Some recent studies confirm that taking your own notes and reviewing them should enhance your performance both on tests of recall and on tests requiring synthesis of lecture information (Maxwell 2).

Reviewing them as soon as possible pays off too. Consider using that hour between classes (or even five minutes of it) to glance back over your notes. What seemed perfectly clear when you wrote it may grow increasingly mysterious as time passes, so review as soon as possible. Copying your notes over may reinforce your memory.

Some students ask permission to tape lectures. Rather than using a recorder as an alternative to taking notes, consider using it in addition to taking notes.

Memory

College and life require critical thinking for survival; they require the synthesis and application of ideas to create solutions and solve problems. One expert finds any kind of thinking impossible, however, without a certain key ingredient, memory. Harry Lorayne, author of *Super Memory—Super Student*, defends his belief (qtd. in Carter and Kravits 133):

> Memory is the stepping-stone to thinking, because without remembering facts, you cannot think, conceptualize, reason, make decisions, create, or contribute. There is no learning without memory.

Identifying memory as "what lies in the gap between the location of information you need and the understanding and application of that information" (132), Lorayne recommends "efficient gathering" and "organized storage" of information.

Efficient gathering involves listening and concentrating followed by repeating either by writing or by speaking to increase "intake efficiency" (132). To organize your storage, try association, writing, grouping and sequencing, visualizing (make silly mental pictures), and mnemonic devices (132–33).

Memory tips from David Ellis in *Becoming A Master Student* (100–104) also include association techniques such as thinking of another person with the same name when you meet someone; that way you will remember the new person's name more easily.

Similarly, when you cannot recall a detail, review all the related details you *can* recall and the one that eluded you may pop into your mind; for example, Ellis suggests that if you forget your great-aunt's name, recall the name of your great-uncle, and that memory may trigger the missing name to pop into your mind. If a test question stumps you, think of an example your instructor used in class or jot down all the related details you *can* remember, and the elusive one may appear (100, 104).

Ellis also emphasizes *writing* as a memory tool partly because it involves not just the brain but the arm, hand and fingers as well. Writing something down is a form of repetition, the most obvious and the best way to commit something to memory. Reciting and repeating *out loud* also reinforce memory and, like writing, involve more than one of your senses. Make up a song or a silly rhyme to repeat. Imitate the style of an actor or singer. Have some fun while you're working (102).

Old rhymes like "Thirty days hath September" and "*i* before *e* except after *c*" have probably been repeated more times than "Do you swear to tell the truth, the whole truth, and nothing but the truth?" And they really work!

Devise your own ways of remembering. If you typically confuse words like *hear* and *here* or *their* and *there*, develop a plan for remembering. For instance, the word *hear* has the word *ear* in it. The word *their* has the word *heir* in it, and the *heirs* will own something, so it will be *theirs*. Similarly, the words *here* and *there* and *where*, all related to *places*, all have the same *ere* combination in them.

Using information is one of the most effective ways of remembering it because with every use, the "neural pathway" to the information widens and becomes easier to access (Ellis 104). Despite their obvious advantages, technological wonders like calculators and memory dial phone features have allowed our memories to go unexercised. Ralph Waldo Emerson would say that we have "built ourselves a coach but lost the use of our feet."

List three details that you have an easy time remembering.

_____

_____

_____

Why are these easy for you to remember?_____

_____

How can you use your answer to improve your memory in other areas?

Tests

How do you feel about tests? How do tests make you feel?

_____

_____

_____

_____

If your answer involves fear, panic, or nausea, college is the place to overcome those problems! Some of your college courses will involve frequent quiz or test opportunities, but in some of your courses you will probably have fewer tests than you are accustomed to. Having only a final exam is not unheard of in upper level or graduate university courses. Although you may disagree, taking a test can be a very satisfying experience if you are well prepared. Someone has said that failing to prepare is preparing to fail.

Before the Test

To say "Don't cram" is probably a waste of print, but being prepared is simpler if you have been reviewing all along. Students themselves advise against procrastinating. You will know most of your college test dates well in advance. That knowledge will allow you to schedule several appointments with yourself before each test date.

Divide your material into small study blocks. Make flash cards. (Forestry instructor Dave Meador writes test questions daily after class. You could make a few flash cards daily as you review your notes and as you read your assignments. Then when test time approaches, you'd have a ready supply of details like formulas, dates, or definitions to study.)

Study in short periods. Several sessions of an hour or a half-hour should be more productive than a marathon. Take a break for your body's sake to stretch or walk through the house or around the block or even around the library if you're there.

Never stay up all night before a test or exam; you may fall asleep while you're taking it! (This has happened.) Just as frightening is the possibility of falling asleep near the end of an attempted all-nighter, oversleeping, and missing the test entirely. (This has happened, too.) Get a good night's rest. WCC nursing students say "Well rested—well tested."

Reviewing once more early in the morning works well for many people. College students are not famous for eating breakfast, but eating something nutritious before a test is advisable. Nursing students say that glucose is brain food!

Having some quiet time immediately before the test may not be possible if your classes are scheduled back to back, but taking a few deep breaths, closing your eyes for a few moments, saying a prayer, or all of the above may help to calm you.

Some students miss a class to study for a test at the next hour. Think twice before you do that. If you have prepared properly and have not procrastinated, what you think you gain on the test may cost you dearly in the class you cut.

During the Test

When you arrive at the classroom, don't let yourself be intimidated or confused by the last-minute discussions of other students. Be positive and confident.

Don't be intimidated *during* the test, either, by students who finish early. Maybe they don't know as much as you do! Maybe they skipped a section. Feel free to use all the time allotted. If you do finish early, rest for a moment and then use the rest of the time to glance back over your test, making sure you have not omitted any problem, question, or section.

One more antidote to test anxiety: this test may seem like the most important thing in the world at this moment, but in the big scheme of things, think of the worst thing that could ever happen in your life, and the answer probably does not even involve this one test grade. Putting events in perspective is always helpful.

When the instructor hands you the test, resist the impulse to start immediately. After any verbal instructions or advice by the instructor, look over the whole test before you begin. The two or three minutes you spend doing this will pay dividends, helping you to budget your time as well as plan ahead for essay choices or your most difficult sections.

Most instructors indicate the value of each section or each question; pay attention to the point values. Using over half the period for twenty one-pointers when essays worth eighty points await your attention would be quite foolish. Scanning the whole test may also provide information useful to you in another section. Budgeting your time may be one of your hardest test jobs. New college students often express surprise at the *length*, not necessarily the *difficulty*, of college tests.

One important reminder is a rule you learned in kindergarten: PUT YOUR NAME ON YOUR PAPER! In fact, put your name on all your pages. Use ink unless your instructor approves pencil, and write only on the front side of the paper unless your instructor approves the back. Be sure to observe any instructions such as "Do not write on the test" or "Write your essay on the back of this page."

After the Test

When the test is over, move on. Don't worry yourself sick about what you did or didn't do, should or shouldn't have done. Apply those lessons to the *next* test. The energy you waste worrying about the test could be better spent working on the next assignment! (I wish I had the statistics to support my theory that most good students actually do *better* than they thought they did on the test, not worse.)

When you get your test back, use it as another learning opportunity. Be sure to examine it carefully to see what you missed and why. (You may even find a grading error to negotiate tactfully with your instructor.)

Grading tests and other papers takes an enormous amount of an instructor's time; returning them as soon as possible while devoting as much care and attention to grading as you did to taking the test is a major concern of most faculty members. To see a student merely glance at the grade without studying the markings and comments is frustrating and disappointing to an instructor who knows that a test is a learning tool. A test on material that you had never studied before beginning the course is also a reminder of how very much new knowledge you have been exposed to. Grades are important, but they may not always fully reveal what you have gained from a course.

Types of Test Questions

You probably know the basic tip for tackling any type of test question:

- *Read the directions.*
- *Read the directions.*
- *Read the directions.*

Multiple Choice

Multiple-choice questions (sometimes called "multiple guess" or "multiple hope") may require more critical thinking than some students realize. Read the directions. Sometimes the directions ask for the *best* answer, indicating that more than one answer is correct and requiring you to analyze the choices carefully.

Ellis (165) suggests trying to complete the statement on your own before looking at the choices; if your firm response is on the list, you can avoid the confusion and conflict of weighing all the answers against each other. If you do not have a preconceived sure answer, use the process of elimination on incorrect and illogical choices. Be cautious about "all of the above" and "none of the above." Skip the puzzling items temporarily; you may find information in subsequent items that will shed light on the ones you have skipped (Long and Ritter 105).

The following clues may help on some tests: all answers should be about the same length, but the correct option may be the longest one; the correct answer may be more precise than the others because of a word like *often*; the correct answer is probably not first or last and, if a number, is probably not the highest or the lowest; an opposite statement or a statement nearly the same as the correct answer may appear on the list; the correct answer probably will not have any unfamiliar technical wording (Holkeboer 7.12).

True-False

True-False questions offer a fifty-fifty chance for a correct answer but can be tricky. Every part of the statement has to be true, and qualifiers such as *always, never,* and *only* suggest false answers while terms like *often* and *frequently* suggest true (Long and Ritter 105). Holkeboer reminds that "if a statement is not completely true, it is false. If a statement is not completely false, it is still false" (7.12).

Matching

Instructors use matching questions to test you on details like terms, names, or dates. Check to see whether the two columns have the same number of choices so you will know whether any responses must go unselected. Start with the column containing the longer entries (definitions or explanations) because scanning the column of brief items looking for the proper term is quicker than scanning the column of complex entries over and over (Walther 156–157). Check off or line through items as you use them.

Be careful about your handwriting; if your lowercase g and q look alike, use capitals. Don't make your instructor try to read your mind or decipher your handwriting; make your letters unmistakable.

I.D. and Definition

Identification items and definitions usually need only brief answers yet with enough detail to distinguish the item from others on the list (Holkeboer 7.14). You can do completion and filling in the blank as fast as you can write if you have really learned or "overlearned" the material (Ellis 166).

Math and Science Tests

Math and science problems demand special test techniques; Ellis (176) suggests translating problems into words, checking your work by doing the opposite operation, using "time drills" while you are studying, analyzing each problem carefully looking for shortcuts, estimating the answer before you start, making "a picture" if you have a mental block, writing the formulas you will need at the top of the test paper as soon as your instructor lets you begin. (Clear that final one with your instructor in advance.) Take advantage of any opportunities for test preparation such as the practice sessions for lab practicals offered by the science faculty here at WCC. See page 116 for a math teacher's tips.

Essays

Essay questions present a different kind of challenge. This chapter on study skills does not address the writing process because every student will take at least one composition course. (Look for the Writing Center described in the "Help" chapter.) Apply all the principles of English 090 or English 111 to every essay test you take. One exception: a test setting does not usually allow time for a very fully developed introduction.

The wording of the question or topic will determine the method of development and the kind of details you include in your essay. The question may require an approach such as to define, compare, contrast, illustrate, prove, explain a process, examine the causes, or list. Be sure to do whatever the question tells you to do. Underlining the topic and the specific instructions will help you to focus (Long and Ritter 100).

Just as time surveying the whole test before you begin pays dividends, so does the time spent in some quick prewriting; brainstorming and making an informal outline will simplify your process, save you time, and allow you to make the essay at least reasonably complete should you begin to run short of time. The earlier advice about budgeting your time bears repeating. Pleas of "ran out of time" will not usually earn any points with an instructor (even when writing on the *carpe diem* theme on a poetry test!), so budget your time.

More Test Tips

Your instructor will probably tell you what the test will be like, so the test should not present any real surprises. As you study, consider the types of questions the instructor announced, and try to anticipate what the specific questions will be. List the terms you assume you will have to match, or predict the essay topics most likely to be included on the test.

One more time, READ THE DIRECTIONS. Many an *A* test paper loses that coveted status when its writer overlooks a section or chooses only *one* essay topic instead of *two*. Some students, on the other hand, fail to read the directions and try to answer *everything* when actually they are supposed to choose from the list of topics.

Please remember that your instructor *wants* you to do well on tests. Simply put, it's much easier to grade a good test paper than a poor one. Instructors also find it gratifying to know that students have learned something, and reading good test answers can be one of the real pleasures of teaching.

Now, list the tests you have already taken this semester. How did you score on each one? What can you do differently if you want a higher score next time?

Test:

Score:

Plans for improvement:

Test:

Score:

Plans for improvement:

Test:

Score:

Plans for improvement:

How Do You Learn Best?

Are you familiar with the concept of learning styles? Formal surveys can reveal your style, but basically, you can determine your own dominant style by thinking about how you learn best.

If you do well listening to lectures, taking notes, reading notes aloud, perhaps taping your instructor's lecture (with permission, of course), you are probably an auditory learner. (Can you hear the voices from your past echoing in your head? Some students say they have an easy time identifying quotations on a literature test because they hear the instructor's voice reading and discussing the passage.)

If you like for instructors to outline their lectures on the board or in a handout, you remember best what you see on graphs or charts or in print, and you learn by copying your notes over, you are probably a visual learner.

Many people learn best by doing, by hands-on activity. Like all labels, these are deceptively simple; most people learn best by a combination of techniques.

Being aware of your dominant learning style can help you adjust to an instructor's teaching style. If you are more visual but your instructor lectures almost exclusively, compensate. Take the best notes possible, coordinate them with your textbook, make flash cards, and you will have visual cues to reinforce the lecture.

If you are more auditory, ask permission to tape the lecture so that you can play it back at will. Tape your own voice reading important material. (Tapes help with time management also, allowing you to "study" while commuting if you have a tape player in your car.) You will learn very quickly your instructor's method; then you can be prepared to get the most out of class time.

Where you sit in class is important. Although the back wall may emit a magnetic attraction, studies show that students who sit at or near the front usually make better grades. Distractions are fewer, the view of the board is better, and hearing the instructor is easier.

One student has pointed out that she began having difficulty in her second class with her same instructor after a highly successful previous course; it took her several days to realize that because she had not arrived in time to claim her favorite spot in the classroom on the first day, she was at a disadvantage trying to see the board from a different angle even though the instructor was writing his same direction and speed!

The Study Skills Course and Other Helps

Ask your advisor about taking College Study Skills (ACA 118), a three-credit-hour course designed especially to improve the success rate of students in English 080, Math 060, and Reading 080 and of students who feel a need to enhance their study skills. You may want to consult some of the study skills materials on campus on your own even if you do not take the course. The Career Center has the popular and effective film *Where There's a Will There's an A* that you may want to see. The ACA 111 reserve materials in the library include numerous texts such as *Becoming a Master Student* by David Ellis; ask at the circulation desk.

Seven

The Library: Make It Your Home Away from Home

Earlier you read a quotation from Cicero: "A room without books is like a body without a soul." Similar analogies surely apply to the library: higher education without a library is like a body without heart or lungs, like a building without windows.

Almost every list of tips for college students from other students, from faculty, or from orientation textbooks mentions the importance of the library. To "fall in love with the library" is a priority for the professor who published his letters to his daughter (Lawry 23). Do not delay. Visit the WCC Library! Your ACA 111 class will tour the library, and one or more of your English classes will probably include a specialized tour, but there is no substitute for spending time there on your own.

This beautiful circular facility on the third floor of the LC Building offers you much. Study areas range from individual carrels to tables (the area across the atrium from the circulation desk is reserved for quietest study) to comfortable balcony areas overlooking the atrium (great for group study). Try to develop a library habit for studying, especially if your home environment has many distractions. Spending an hour between classes studying in the library atmosphere may be more productive than several hours somewhere else. (Would you spend a week at the beach without looking at the ocean? Going to college without considering the library for your study place makes about that much sense!)

Knowledgeable and helpful staff members want you to interrupt them! The automated catalog gives you access to an impressive collection of books (42,000± at last count) and indexes more than a million items through the CCLINC network (Community College Libraries in North Carolina, a statewide network of forty community college libraries). The catalog can tell you whether a book is checked out and for how long and even allows you to put a hold on the book so the library staff can call you when the book is turned in. Did you know that instructors have access to the automated catalog through the computer terminals in their offices? This feature really facilitates student-instructor discussions of paper topics and research materials. The catalog is available online at http://www.cclinc.ncccs. cc.nc.us/webclientwy.html for users with web access.

An impressive general collection and reference collection will meet your needs for almost any topic you ever need to research during your college career. (Did you know Ben Franklin founded the first public subscription library to give people access to more books than they could afford on their own? If only he could see how many books you have access to in your college library!) Do you subscribe to a newspaper or magazine at home? The library increases your subscriptions to at least 330 magazines and 15 newspapers!

Those are only a fraction of the materials available through electronic access at the more than a dozen Internet stations in your library. NC LIVE (North Carolina Libraries and Virtual Education) is a collaborative effort of the State Library, the North Carolina Community College System, the University of North Carolina, public libraries, and some private colleges to provide electronic access to information. It is funded by an appropriation from the General Assembly and is available over the Internet to computers located in public and academic libraries.

NC LIVE provides access to EBSCOhost, ProQuest, FirstSearch, PsycINFO, and NoveList. EBSCOhost, Gale InfoTrac, and ProQuest contain large numbers of full-text articles from magazines, journals, and newspapers which can be downloaded to a disc or printed out. Both also index many periodicals not carried in full text. FirstSearch and PsycINFO provide additional indexing to several thousand publications. By using NC LIVE for research, you have some assurance that your Internet sources have been screened for reliability.

The library's Web page (http://www.wayne.cc.nc.us/library/wcclib.htm) has a link to Internet citation information to help you document your findings correctly.

Even Ben Franklin's kite and key trick did not prepare him for what he would see in your library! More electronic communication links all the libraries in Wayne County to each other and to the State Library. The WCC Library is the host site for this link called WIN, the Wayne Information Network.

Interlibrary Loan allows you to borrow materials from statewide and regional libraries; be sure to allow enough advance notice, and ask the librarian about possible cost for this service, but this is another way that your own access is multiplied a thousand times!

Inquire at the circulation desk about the Vertical File of pamphlets, maps, and clippings available for use in the library and the collection of more than 5,000 audiovisual items. Also at the circulation desk is a box containing cards for all the books instructors have removed from circulation because of students' concentrated need for them in various courses; always check the reserve box as soon as you begin your search for materials for a paper or project. FAX and copy machines are available for your use also.

State-of-the-art access to a wealth of materials awaits you in the library. Your WCC ID card properly barcoded at the circulation desk is your ticket. When can you go? The library is open many hours:

Monday–Thursday	7:45 A.M. until 9:00 P.M.
Friday	7:45 A.M. until 5:00 P.M.
Saturday	10:00 A.M. until 2:00 P.M.

Summer hours may vary.
Changes for holidays and breaks will be announced.

Visit the library's home page at http://www.wayne.cc.nc.us/library/wcclib.htm if you wish.

Open a window to the world. Activate the pulse and breath of your college education. Go to the library!

(A special thanks to Dr. Shirley Jones, Susan Parris, Donna Potter, Dot Elledge, and the whole library staff for the many tours and presentations provided for ACA 111 classes and to Dot Elledge for coordinating tours and consulting on this chapter)

Chapter Eight

Student Activities: Be a Part, Not Apart

This whole book is about *you*; this whole college is about *you*; and the *student* in "Student Activities" and "Student Government Association" is definitely *you*. Studies show that students who get involved in campus activities have lower dropout rates. No matter how busy you are, you can find an organization or activity to be a part of on campus.

Students who are registered for six or more semester hours during Fall and Spring Semesters pay an activity fee of $16.00 per semester. The fee is prorated for part-time students. (The North Carolina legislature dictates maximum student activity fees including parking fees.)

Student identification cards for students who have paid the activity fee are used for the library card (must be properly bar coded on the back at the circulation desk), for admission to cookouts and dances, for participation in intramural sports, for check cashing (although an automatic teller machine near the cashier's window in the LC Atrium has eliminated the need for personal check cashing), for bookstore and business office use, and for general identification on campus. Present your student ID at the Student Activities Office to get a pass to the Family Y for the day. (First come, first served.)

Have your picture ID made in the Student Activities office between the LC Atrium and the Student Lounge as soon as you have registered and paid your tuition and fees; keep your receipt as proof to get your card made. Your handbook calendar contains the schedule for having ID cards made. Your card is valid until you graduate; simply have it stamped each semester when you pay your fees. If you lose your card, you can get a replacement for $5.00.

The *Student Handbook* contains the constitution and bylaws of SGA. Membership in SGA includes "all students who pay the activity fee." The Student Activities Coordinator serves as Student Government Advisor. Elections for the executive branch of SGA leadership are held Spring Semester. Enrollment for the previous semester, a 2.75 grade point average, and a petition containing 100 student signatures are the requirements for candidacy. Officers receive a tuition scholarship for Fall through Summer. The legislative branch of SGA leadership (Student Council) includes three representatives from each academic department and three from each approved student club. (Check your handbook for more specific details.)

Every curriculum student at WCC is welcome to attend SGA meetings. Only representative delegates can vote, but all students can have their say. An open forum during the last fifteen minutes of each meeting allows students to voice their opinions on college issues.

Identify your SGA leadership by finding names and photos in your *Student Handbook*:

Student Government Advisor and Coordinator_____

SGA President _____

SGA Vice President _____

SGA Secretary _____

Other Officers _____

Your SGA sponsors many special activities on campus such as Spring Fling complete with cookout, drinks, music, early class dismissal, games. It also co-sponsors and helps to fund both social and educational functions for students. Student Activities coordinates a recreational program including intramural basketball, flag football, volleyball, and golf as well as many other intramural sports. Check the trophy case in the atrium near the Student Activities office to learn about some of the athletic achievements of WCC teams.

Clubs at Wayne Community College reflect academic programs as well as special non-academic interests. Check your handbook for information about the International Students' Club, Phi Beta Lambda, Students in Free Enterprise, North Carolina Student Nurses' Association, WCC Student American Dental Hygienists' Association, Multi-Cultural Association for Enrichment, Forestry Club, and Agriculture Club. Check your handbook and watch for publicity about any new clubs that may be organized while you are a student. You may even want to investigate the possibility of initiating your own special interest group such as the African-American Males Committed to Success, which emphasizes confidence and self-esteem for success.

Two kinds of recognition you may receive as an outstanding student are membership in Phi Theta Kappa and membership in Who's Who Among Students at WCC. Phi Theta Kappa, a national organization, recognizes students who achieve a 3.5 grade point average after 16 semester hours in an associate degree curriculum. Who's Who includes about one percent of the whole student body and honors students who have a 2.5 average along with a record of campus and community service.

Student Development sponsors a program of Ambassadors, a group of highly qualified students who represent the college at official functions. Ambassadors receive tuition scholarships and training. Watch for announcements in the spring if you are interested in this program.

Participation and leadership in SGA or any other college organizations can help build good resumes and can strengthen preparation for interviews.

Remember: *YOU* are the student in SGA and other student activities. Fulfill that role to add an element of fun and experience to your college career. Be *a part of*, not *apart from* this vital feature of college life.

(Special thanks to Wayne Parson and Carl Brow for consulting on this section and for their frequent presentations to ACA 111 classes)

Chapter Nine

Health:
Not Just a
Course You Take

Mens sana in corpore sano, "a sound mind in a sound body," describes the ideal college student's condition. How healthy are you? How healthy is your lifestyle?

Most college students are in what should be the healthiest stage of their lives. However, college life lends itself to some potentially unhealthy habits including but not limited to those associated with the social scene. Hectic schedules; fatigue; eating fast food on the run or skipping a meal entirely; losing sleep for studying, work, family responsibilities, or social life; stress (enhanced by all of the above)—these are some of the common enemies of college students' health. Tips in your time management chapter make a good prescription for combating many of these enemies.

What about you? In the past week, have you

- overslept because you stayed up too late (studying, partying, working)? _____
- missed a meal? _____
- eaten fast food? _____
- felt stressed out? _____
- been too tired to do an assignment? _____

Allow time in your schedule to eat and sleep adequately!

If you should become ill while you are in school, are you aware that you have access to a free medical appointment? For an appointment, go to the Student Activities Office around 10:30 on Wednesday, have your vital signs taken, and receive the paperwork that will allow you to see a physician between 11:00 and noon at Healthwise Medical Associates of Goldsboro, 2607 Medical Office Place.

At other hours, the Student Activities Office offers first aid, emergency assistance, and a place to rest if you should become ill on campus.

Are you aware that WCC has a Fitness Center (MSS 207)? Various physical education classes meet there, but it is available many hours weekly for your use. The center is equipped with Stairmaster, stationary bikes, treadmills, universal weights, and free weights. The campus also serves as a beautiful and safe setting for walkers, and six tennis courts offer you another exercise option. Although you may get a little exercise changing classes, work some fitness time into your schedule to combat all the sitting you do for class and study time.

Alcohol, Drugs, and Tobacco

"The best mind-altering drug is truth."

Lily Tomlin, American humorist
(qtd. in Holkeboer 13.20).

A grave traditional threat to the health and success of college students is alcohol and drug abuse.

Recent statistics indicate that one in seven drinkers will become an alcoholic. Alcoholism in the family affects four out of ten Americans; nearly half of all traffic fatalities are alcohol-related; fetal alcohol syndrome is the only preventable one of the top three causes of birth defects (Ellis 280). The fine for a DUI or DWI offense is only the beginning of its actual cost. An impressive percentage of manslaughter convictions, college rapes, and battered spouse cases involve alcohol.

Certain strains of marijuana today are 600 times stronger than the marijuana of the 1960s and 1970s, and the effects of this drug that some people like to consider innocent range from chronically slower reaction time and memory impairment to greater likelihood of respiratory problems and cancer (Mohn, Johnson, Johnson, and King 224). Cocaine in any form is one of the most highly addictive known drugs.

Obviously, any substance not conducive to a safe and successful life has no place in the college environment. Although most people associate excessive college drinking with large residential campuses, studies do show the same kind of negative correlation between drinking and grades among community college students as among university students.

The potential legal problems, health problems, social problems, and academic problems caused by substance abuse of any kind deserve your intelligent and most responsible consideration. Reliable information about the dangers of alcohol, prescription drugs, and illegal drugs may be some of the most important facts you can find in your textbooks or the library.

Alcohol and drug addiction share some features with any other kind of addiction: compulsive use or indulgence; continuing the activity despite the resulting problems; being preoccupied with obtaining the substance or doing whatever the addiction involves; losing control over the substance or activity; promising to stop or cut down but not succeeding (Ellis 282).

Think about your own potential for abuse or addiction. Don't let anything or anybody rob you of control over your own life. The counselors on campus are available to discuss personal as well as academic difficulties, so take advantage of their services.

The WCC Student Code of Conduct found in the *Student Handbook* addresses the possession or use of alcoholic beverages and illegal drugs on campus. A foldout section at the end of the *Student Handbook* identifies the health risks of drugs and alcohol, North Carolina laws regarding drugs and alcohol, prevention and abuse resources, and the college's prevention program and policy.

Former WCC student Michael Herring, now a graduate of ECU, has often spoken to classes about his own experiences and recovery; videotapes of his presentation are on ACA 111 reserve in the library if you are interested. He now teaches in the substance abuse curriculum.

Recognizing the health problems associated with smoking, WCC has a policy of smoke-free buildings. Cigarette smoking is responsible for 87 percent of deaths from lung cancer, according to the American Cancer Society; despite statistics like this one and all the evidence of other smoking-related illnesses, more than 3,000 teenagers in this country become regular smokers daily (Ellis 280). Someone has said that *everyone* is too young to smoke. Never starting is easier than stopping, but stopping is not impossible.

Physicians specializing in ear, nose, and throat offer pregnant women and parents who smoke some especially frightening facts to consider in a brochure called *Secondhand Smoke and Children*. Studies relate smoking during pregnancy to birth defects such as cleft lip or palate and to behavioral problems such as hyperactivity, to lower birth weight for babies, and to lower milk production in nursing mothers. Secondhand smoke can damage developing organs like lungs and brain. It also decreases lung efficiency; impairs lung function; increases frequency and severity of childhood asthma; aggravates various respiratory problems; increases colds, sore throats, and ear infections; and causes cancer. Recent studies link Sudden Infant Death Syndrome, or crib death, to secondhand smoke, according to some sources.

AIDS

AIDS (Acquired Immuno-Deficiency Syndrome) is a solemn concern that college students of the past did not have to consider. There is no cure for this disease, and the death rate is high.

According to the *North Carolina 2000 HIV/AIDS Surveillance Report*, the reported cumulative number of HIV cases diagnosed in Wayne County since 1983 is 303, and the number of AIDS cases, 184. The number of AIDS cases diagnosed in North Carolina from before 1988 through the year 2000 is 10,329. From those reported North Carolina cases, the number of deaths is 5,751.

These local statistics provide a sobering reminder of a worldwide problem. The Center for Disease Control Website gives "International Statistics" furnished by the *Joint United Nations Programme on HIV/AIDS*:

- An estimated 36.1 million people are living with HIV/AIDS; 34.7 million of these are adults (16.4 million of those adults are women, a rapidly increasing number) and 1.4 million are children.

- Deaths of 3 million people in 2000 were attributed to illnesses associated with HIV; children under 15 were 500,000 of them.
  (Statistics updated January 2, 2001)

College students should be aware of a disturbing trend: *The 2000 North Carolina AIDS Index* reports that "nearly ⅓ of all reported HIV cases in North Carolina occur among those in their twenties," suggesting that these patients must have been infected as adolescents (14). According to this publication, 25% of the cases of AIDS reported from 1996 to 1998 were women, and "the number of women diagnosed with AIDS has increased every year since 1990" (13). Treatment and prevention for newborn babies is one of the few encouraging trends cited in the *Index*; the number of infants born with the virus dropped from 25–30% to 3% between 1997 and 2000 because of screening and treatment of pregnant women (13).

The Wayne County Health Department, 301 N. Herman St. (corner of Herman and Ash), administers free blood tests for HIV (human immunodeficiency virus, the cause of AIDS) Monday–Friday, 8:00–4:00. Phone: 731-1000. Anonymity is still an option. Information on an HIV/AIDS support group is also available through the Health Department.

The passage of the AIDS virus occurs through sexual intercourse with an infected person; through sharing of needles or syringes with an infected person; from mother to baby either before, during, or after birth (the latter by breast feeding); or through a contaminated blood supply in transfusion (almost nonexistent today).

People need to remember that the AIDS virus is *NOT* passed by any of the following, according to many reliable sources of information: sitting beside someone with AIDS; touching, shaking hands, a simple social kiss; eating in a restaurant; sharing food, plates, cups, or utensils; using restroom, water fountain, telephone; taking care of someone with AIDS if using proper precautions; donating blood; mosquito or other insect bites.

This killer disease has been the subject of regular seminars at WCC. Dr. Edmond Hogan of our faculty facilitates the seminars; Dr. James Atkins, local oncologist, presents current statistics and information; and AIDS patients and families of AIDS patients or victims appear on a panel. Many students comment on the eye-opening effect of the seminars in providing information and encouraging compassion for victims and their families. You will probably be offered extra credit in some classes for attending this event. Don't miss it.

The Department of Student Development recommends that you take your AIDS questions or concerns to Dr. Ed Hogan, Azalea 314A (extension 276).

Some Other Current Health Threats

Other STD's

Although AIDS is the most obvious threat today, other sexually transmitted diseases demand attention also. The correlation between the others and HIV increases their seriousness: "When exposed to HIV through sexual contact, a person who is infected with other STDs is three to five times more likely to contract HIV than a person without other STDs" (*AIDS Index 31*).

According to information provided by the WCC Nursing Department, North Carolina has some alarming statistics related to sexually transmitted diseases. The number of NC residents infected with gonorrhea, syphilis, and chlamydia increased by 12% between 1983 and 1994. Our state's syphilis rate has been as high in the nineties as before penicillin became available in the 1940's. NC led the nation in the number of gonorrhea cases in both 1994 and 1995. The state ranked fourth in reported syphilis cases in 1994 but jumped to second in 1995—second in the nation despite being only the tenth most populous state. Since a decline in 1996, infection rates for syphilis, gonorrhea and chlamydia in North Carolina have not changed significantly (*AIDS Index 31*). However, 31 counties in the nation account for 50% of the syphilis cases in the nation, and 5 of those counties are in North Carolina (Forsyth, Guilford, Orange, Alamance, and Durham); this high incidence of syphilis places

North Carolina on the "national high morbidity area" list of the Centers for Disease Control (*AIDS Index 31*).

Because their immune system has not matured, young females suffer an increased susceptibility to STD from unprotected sex. Teens and young adults of both sexes are more susceptible to STD infections than older people, and teen patients are particularly likely to pass gonorrhea and other STDs on unknowingly because symptoms do not occur or are too mild to be noticed. In this state, the highest rate of chlamydia is among young people from 13 to 19, and the highest rate of gonorrhea is among those 20 to 29 years old (*AIDS Index 31*).

With potential long-range effects including fetal infection, risk of infertility, and increased susceptibility to HIV infection, sexually transmitted diseases deserve serious concern and informed awareness on the part of college students.

Hepatitis

According to the Nursing Department, hepatitis or inflammation of the liver has multiple causes including the viral infection called Hepatitis B. It is the main infectious health hazard in the health care field. Students in Allied Health programs as well as the many students employed in health care facilities, law enforcement, and fire and rescue agencies are at high risk of contracting Hepatitis B because of their frequent exposure to blood and other contaminated body fluids.

Certain lifestyles also increase the risk of contracting this potentially fatal liver condition: the lifestyle of people who inject illegal drugs and that of people who have more than one sexual partner in a period of six months.

Although there is no cure, there is a vaccine to prevent hepatitis B. Sixth graders in Wayne County Schools receive the vaccine. Pediatricians urge college students to take the series of three shots, and health care workers of course need the series.

Tuberculosis

Once the leading cause of death in the United States, tuberculosis nearly disappeared from American society for several decades but has made a comeback since 1984 (*Q&A 1*). It is spread through the air from person to person (1). The bacteria most often attack the lungs and may produce chest pain and a productive cough (3). People with weak immune systems such as those with HIV are especially vulnerable (7)

A skin test at the health department or doctor's office is the only way to determine whether someone is infected (*Q&A 5*). Who should be tested? Testing is important for all people who have been around someone with the infection, all who have a weakened immune system, all who suspect they have the disease, all who are from a country with a high incidence of the disease, all who inject drugs, and all who live in any of the places where exposure is likely such as "most homeless shelters, migrant farm camps, prisons and jails, and some nursing homes" (5).

Both preventive therapy and treatment for the disease are available. Anyone infected should take the obvious precautions of taking all medication, exercising good hygiene (covering mouth and nose when coughing or sneezing or even laughing, carefully disposing of tissues), avoiding public places and close contact with others, and airing rooms (13).

Stress

Of all the potential health problems mentioned in these pages, stress is the one that everybody experiences. Stress is not unnatural, and a certain amount of stress serves to motivate. However, an accumulation of stresses can actually make you sick. Coping with stress is a necessary survival skill in college and in life.

- Has anything stressful happened to you today? What was it?

_____

_____

- How did it make you feel?

_____

_____

- Did you have any control over it?

_____

- List some other sources of stress in your life:

_____

_____

_____

_____

_____

_____

Does your list include any financial items? school-related items? work-related items? responsibilities? relationships?

Change is a major cause of stress. Even positive changes, happy occasions like marriage or a great new job or retirement or an honor, involve stress. Any new adventure like starting college involves stress, partly because of the unfamiliar or the unknown. Psychologists often assign a point value to life events and changes to evaluate stress levels. List any major changes you have experienced during the past year such as a death in the family, a job change, a change in marital status, a move, graduating from high school, transferring from another school. Be sure to include starting college at WCC!

_____

_____

_____

_____

_____

How have these changes affected your life? How well have you handled the changes? Some people say they can handle life's big problems, but it's the little things that slip up on them and stress them out. Managing your stress is possible. It requires some of the same tactics as time management.

- Avoid stress if you can. (Maybe you cannot do something extreme like quitting your job, but anticipating a stressful situation can help you prepare for it.)

- Plan ahead.

- Don't procrastinate.

- Talk to someone about what is stressing you out.

- Eat properly and sleep enough.

- Get regular exercise.

- Learn to say "no" pleasantly if you do not have time to do something someone asks you to do.

- Lighten up. Put your stress in perspective. If this is the worst thing that ever happens to you, aren't you quite fortunate?

- "This too shall pass" has been the motto of many a struggling student.

- Take a break from your study or work to do something physical like walk around the block or roll your shoulders.

- Take a five-minute vacation (or an afternoon vacation or even a weekend if you can afford to).

- Counselor Sharon Price advises, "Don't spend ten dollars' worth of stress on a ten-cent problem."

- Remember that you are not in charge of the whole world.

Healthy LIFEstyle

Take care of yourself! A sound mind in a sound body is as essential for success in college as textbooks and study skills. It is also as essential for *life* as it is for *college* life.

NOTE: The title of this chapter, "Health: Not Just A Course You Take," reminds you that health is much more than a class.

However, WCC does indeed offer several valuable health or physical education courses required for graduation. Personal Health and Wellness, Community Health, and First Aid and CPR offer three hours each. The activity courses (prefix PED for physical education) include swimming, bowling, tennis, weight training, aerobics, and softball. Enhance your health, fitness, and recreation by taking health and fitness courses.

If you have served in the military, inquire in Admissions and Records about automatic credit for physical education courses, but don't forget to provide yourself some exercise opportunities anyway.

Present your ID in Student Activities for a Family Y pass (first come–first served) for the day or weekend.

(Special thanks to Dr. Cindy Archie; nursing instructors Ludia Burden, Patty Elgin, and Caroline Phillips; Dot Elledge; Mike Saylors; Betsey Pritchett; Josie Raynor, Wayne County Health Department; and to Carl Brow, Michael Herring, and Jerry Penuel for presentations)

Chapter Ten

Don't Drop Out Because of Money; Drop in at Financial Aid

The Financial Aid Office is on first floor LC. You can enter through the double doors to the left of the elevators or through the double doors to the right of the cashier's window near the atrium stairs or from the hallway that passes through the counselors' area.

Yvonne Goodman, Associate Vice President for Student Development, is also Financial Aid Director. She and her staff encourage every student to fill out the *Free Application for Federal Student Aid.* The Student Aid Report that you will receive after mailing in this application can be used to determine your eligibility for state and local aid as well. During the 2000–2001 school year, the WCC Financial Aid office provided financial assistance to more than 1,600 students. If you have not filled out the application, it may not be too late; Pell Grant funds can be awarded retroactively, so you could still be reimbursed for this semester. Your (or your parents') tax forms for last year are necessary for completing the application. Financial Aid staff are well informed and able to help you with any special situation that might have arisen that changes your family's financial status and with many details that you would consider a threat to your eligibility.

You do not have to be a full-time student to receive financial aid. Twelve hours is considered a full-time course load to be eligible for aid as a full-time student; however, taking even three hours allows students to receive partial funding.

Avoid comparing your eligibility to that of any other student because even a husband and wife may be eligible for different amounts of aid. Each person's aid is based on numerous factors making eligibility an individual matter.

Several loan programs such as the Stafford Loan can assist students, but our financial aid officials discourage students from accepting loans if grants and scholarships are available simply because the loans must eventually be repaid beginning six months after graduating, leaving school, or dropping below half-time enrollment, perhaps before students have reached financial stability. Students who do have loans through federal student aid are required to attend periodic counseling sessions on campus.

The Federal Pell Grant is the main form of aid for WCC students. It is called an entitlement program because it provides funds for every eligible student. If you have a Pell Grant, read CAMNET for announcements telling when you may pick up your check supplying the remainder of your grant after all of your academic expenses for the semester have been paid. The Pell Grant will pay up to a maximum of 150 percent of the hours attempted in an academic program of study. That number includes courses that you drop, so be cautious with decisions to drop classes.

Another important source of aid at WCC is the Federal Supplemental Educational Opportunity Grant (FSEOG) for students with exceptional financial need. This grant can be awarded to a student who also has a Pell Grant.

The Federal Work-Study Program is a popular form of financial aid. Students earn money by working on campus, usually in an area related to their field of study. Job performance is evaluated, and work-study can be listed as work experience on a resume. Many WCC work-study students eventually become full-time employees after completing their education. (Ms. Goodman herself was a work-study student a few years ago!) Work-study students are popular with faculty, staff, and administration for their help. Look around in various departments and you will notice students busily working. Their working hours are scheduled around their classes, and many work as much as fifteen hours a week. Pay is at least minimum wage, and the advantages of working on campus rather than leaving for another workplace after or between classes are obvious. Work-study income does not penalize a student's eligibility the next year. Studies show that students who are involved in campus activities including work-study rarely drop out.

You will find all this information and more in a little booklet called *The Student Guide* available in the Financial Aid Office.

Other Grants and Scholarships

Students who do not qualify for a Pell Grant should inquire about the North Carolina Community College Grant. The North Carolina Student Incentive Grant is a special grant that must be applied for by February 15 for the next school year. Students must be enrolled full-time to receive these funds.

Other forms of aid at WCC include local scholarships. The Foundation of Wayne Community College provided more than $134,500 in scholarships for 2000–2001, thanks to many generous citizens and corporate citizens like Wooten Oil Co. Meet Executive Director of the Foundation Jack Kannan in Dogwood 137. Read CAMNET announcements in April and May for a whole group of scholarships from the Foundation, the North Carolina Department of Community Colleges, and companies like Southern Bell and CP&L. These scholarships sometimes go unclaimed because students do not apply. YOU SHOULD APPLY! Organizations such as local home extension clubs offer scholarships, and the Wayne Community College Association of Educational Office Professionals offers a $250 award each semester.

Many scholarships target a specific group of students; Orville Redenbacher, for example, offers 25 scholarships of $1,000 each to students 30 years old or older. More than 400,000 scholarships are listed on the Internet at the following website: www.fastweb.com

Our Financial Aid Office has staff members to work with veterans' benefits and with the child-care program as well as special emergency funds.

Beyond the Financial Aid Office, other monetary resources include the Workforce Investment Act (WIA), an individual referral program (when funding is available).

Another source of assistance is Vocational Rehabilitation. Goldsboro has two offices (check your phone book). You do not have to have an obvious disability to be eligible for VR assistance; students with documented severe asthma or learning disabilities may be served through this program. Counselor Lee Brettmann can advise these students.

The requirement of academic success for keeping your financial aid is based on a sliding scale found in your student handbook. Your required grade point average is not so demanding your first semester but rises each semester in recognition of the 2.0 grade point average required for graduation. If you must drop a class or withdraw from school, be sure to process an official drop form so as not to jeopardize your good standing for financial aid in the future. You must complete at least 67 percent of the hours you attempt each academic year to remain in good standing with Financial Aid.

Someone from Financial Aid will speak to your ACA 111 class and will be able to answer all your questions. The amount of aid available is good news!

Don't let money problems discourage you from finishing college. Help is as near as the Financial Aid Office!

(Special thanks to Yvonne Goodman and her staff for their many presentations in ACA 111 classes and for consulting on this chapter)

HELP!
(Another Important Four-Letter Word)

You've heard about financial help available at WCC. You've heard about medical help. Almost any other kind of help you could need is here for the asking. Earlier parts of this book have considered important four-letter words like *self* and *time*, but perhaps just as important is the word *help*, especially your willingness to ask for it when you need it. Years ago on the old campus, a very discouraged student learned from her instructor about all the resources available to help her. She exclaimed, "Then *nobody* should fail here." Wayne Community College prides itself on offering multiple options for student assistance. All you have to do is ask for and accept the help. A more recent student expressed awe that all of the *help* is *free!*

Know Your Advisor!

Probably your earliest correspondence from Wayne Community College told you of your acceptance and also told you the name of your academic advisor. How appropriate for that person to be one of the first people mentioned to you! Let that be a reminder that your academic advisor is the first person to consult when you need advice or help. Make a point of getting to know your advisor. Learn where the office is and what the office hours are each semester. To wait until time for phone or on-campus preregistration for the second semester to visit your advisor is to ignore one of your greatest resources. Unless you have your advisor for an instructor, your time together will be limited to working on schedules, checking on graduation and transfer requirements, and discussing your academic progress UNLESS you take time to get to know your advisor.

Look at the tips from students in Chapter 14. More than one student gave this kind of advice: "Learn who your advisor is and become friends with him or her," and "Stay in touch with your advisor."

At the end of this chapter is an assignment that your College Student Success instructor will make to remind you to see your academic advisor early in the semester!

Help! Academic Assistance!

The first avenue for the student who is having academic difficulty is, of course, **the instructor**. Instructors have regular office hours when they can work with you and suggest additional resources. (Write these office hours in your notebook the first day of class or keep the handout your instructor gives you the first day.) If you have the slightest reservation about going to see your instructor, turn to the list of tips from instructors near the end of this book. You will notice that instructors are very human, very willing to help; most of them even have a good sense of humor! All of them want you to succeed.

Still not convinced? Well, college is like the rest of the world: we often have to do things we are not completely comfortable doing, and we usually discover that we have wasted energy on fear and dread. Go see your instructor right away when you need help! (As a matter of fact, several faculty members submitted that very tip for the list in your book.)

Academic Skills Center

The Academic Skills Center located on third floor LC (east side of the library facility) offers academic support through individualized instruction and materials like workbooks, worksheets, audio and video cassettes, computer software, interactive video, and CD-ROM programs. Director Saundra Smith and other staff members offer individual and small-group assistance. Referral by instructor and computer log-in allow you to get help in reading, English, math, science, business, computer, and other college subjects. Another helpful service, test make-up, is coordinated between ASC and your instructors.

ASC is open Monday–Thursday from 7:45 A.M. to 9:00 P.M.; Friday from 7:45 A.M. to 5:00 P.M.; and Saturday from 10:00 A.M. to 2:00 P.M. (No testing is done on Saturday, but all other services are available.) Summer hours may vary.

Peer Tutors

The Academic Skills Center is also the place to apply for a tutor if you need regular help with any course. As with all the sources of academic help, don't delay. Ask for help as soon as you realize you need it! If you are a top student in any discipline, inquire about becoming a tutor. Tutoring is free, but tutors get paid!

The Writing Center

Working on a paper? If you need help with organization, development, grammar, punctuation, research, documentation, or word processing, visit the Writing Center on the mezzanine (fourth floor) of LC. Enter by the stairway near the circulation desk of the library. On your first visit each semester, you must complete the referral form near the computers. (Your instructor can send the referral with you, or the Writing Center staff will send the form to your instructor for a signature.) Although walk-ins are assisted when possible, signing up for an appointment is strongly recommended, especially at times during the quarter when many papers are due. You may make an appointment for writing assistance or for computer use.

The Writing Center can help you with any writing project, not just for English classes, as long as your instructor approves. You need to bring the text you are writing from or about; pen, pencil, paper; a 3.5" or 5.25" diskette if you plan to use the computers frequently; and specific details from your instructor about the assignment. Allow plenty of time between your visit and your deadline; don't wait until the day before the paper is due!

Sharon Royal, Director, and the other English instructors on duty at the Writing Center will not write your outline or paper for you, of course, nor will they guarantee an *A*, but the assistance they provide is sure to enhance your process and your product. Hours are posted all over campus and on CAMNET each semester and include Monday–Friday hours, some evening hours, and Saturday morning hours some semesters.

Basic Skills Computer Lab

The Basic Skills Computer Lab is a free computerized educational program on the first floor of Pine Building. Coordinator Denece Berry and her staff are available to help, but you need no computer skills, and you work at your own pace and at your own level; your assigned password assures confidentiality, so you need not feel embarrassed if you prefer to begin at a very elementary level for your academic skills review. Many students use this facility to prepare for placement tests or to maintain their skills if they skip a semester between certain math courses, for example. Programs include basic math and calculus, chemistry, English grammar and composition, resume writing and interview skills.

No appointment is necessary. Watch CAMNET for lab hours. Filling out a simple form on your first visit admits you to the program, and your instructor will complete a referral form for the record. This facility is open to the community as well as students. Many visitors use it to prepare for tests such as the Graduate Record Exam.

Other Labs

The Open Computer Lab in Magnolia 215 has very generous hours. It stays open 8:00 A.M.–8:00 P.M. Monday–Thursday, 8:00 A.M.–5:00 P.M. Friday, and 10:00 A.M.–4:00 P.M. Saturday. (Summer hours vary.) This lab has fifty computers, almost every kind of software used for classes on this campus, Internet access, and e-mail. Tutors from the Academic Skills Center's peer tutor program are available in this lab.

The Accounting Lab in the Business/Computer Technology Division on second floor LC is available for accounting students. Hours are posted each semester.

Check with instructors for other special lab or workshop opportunities available.

Help! Counseling!

One of the first people you met on campus was probably a counselor in Student Development, first floor of LC Building. Counselors interview entering students and assist with enrolling, registering, placement assessment, and program information.

While you are a student here, counselors are available 8:00 A.M.–5:00 P.M. Monday–Friday and Monday and Wednesday untill 7:00 P.M. to give you guidance on personal, career, and academic concerns. Just walk in and a counselor will see you as soon as possible.

Although each counselor has specific responsibilities, all the counselors want you to feel free to ask them for help. Susan Keel, Director of Counseling Services, is academic advisor for many entering students who have not declared a major.

Carl Brow is the official counselor for students seeking entrance to the limited admissions programs in Allied Health. Like many other staff and faculty members, this man has much in common with you because a few years ago he was a student here and graduated from two WCC programs, Automotive and College Transfer. Then he transferred to East Carolina University for his four-year degree, taught in Japan, and returned to ECU for a master's degree. Knowing that Mr. Brow and others on staff were students here should make you feel very comfortable asking for help. The expression "They've been there" is more than just a figure of speech!

Lee Brettmann, Counselor/Disability Services, assists students who have documented disabilities, providing them with reasonable academic accommodations. Financial Aid officials recommend that you see Ms. Brettmann for additional financial information if you have a disability.

Sharon Price, the counselor who specializes in college transfer, can provide you with instant information on transferring to most four-year schools in the state as well as requirements for specific programs at those schools. See her to make sure you are following your Curriculum Guidelines (see Chapter 12) to satisfy the college to which you intend to transfer as well as WCC. Ms. Price arranges for the most popular transfer universities to send someone to our campus for individual appointments with our students. Watch CAMNET for the appointment schedule. College Day brings representatives from four-year schools to the atrium in another opportunity for you to get first-hand information at no expense. Don't miss these chances to make transferring simpler.

One additional note to College Transfer students: You will be happy to learn that WCC's transfers into the UNC system have traditionally achieved third and fourth year GPAs that compare very favorably with those of students who have taken their first two years in UNC schools. You can also be glad that articulation agreements between the UNC system and the NC Community College System have simplified the transfer process.

A counselor sometimes on duty in Student Development, but more often in the Career Center, is Norma Dawson. Read about her special assistance with your future in the next section.

Janice Fields is a counselor who also has recruiting duties. Like many others in Student Development, Ms. Fields may appear in your ACA 111 class as a speaker or even as your instructor!

Student Development offers other special events like Alcohol Awareness Week and Wellness Day, when you can get cholesterol readings, body fat content, and many other medical tests absolutely free. Watch CAMNET for details.

Help! The Future!

Life after WCC may include transferring to a four-year school, going to work, or both.

- Do you intend to continue in your present job? _____

- Do you plan to graduate from WCC? _____

- If so, from what program? _____

- Do you plan to go on to a four-year school? _____

- Do you plan to go to graduate school? _____

- What kind of job would make you happiest? _____

- What kind of work are you best suited for? _____

- What is a higher priority for you: financial reward or personal satisfaction?
  _____

- Do you prefer to remain in this area, or would you be interested in moving to a different part of the state or country? _____

Questions like these are important to consider! Thoreau writes in "Life Without Principle" about making a living: "It is remarkable that there is little to be remembered written on the subject of getting a living: how to make getting a living not merely honest and honorable, but altogether inviting and glorious; for if getting a living is not so, then living is not." In his poem "Listen Up," WCC graduate Michael B. Jones warns against the same tragedy when he writes of "the punch-clock rhythm of wasted life." Don't let it happen to you! Don't settle for less than a fulfilling career!

Obviously, a major motive for most college students is to prepare for a career, to get ready to make a living. Financial security is one real necessity; personal satisfaction is another. Knowing why you are here, where you want to go from here, what you want to do with your life, and what you want out of life has much to do with what happens while you are here. WCC offers many services to help you identify the career that will make your life's work—and your life—as Thoreau describes it, "honest and honorable . . . inviting and glorious."

One of the best places to go to consider these concepts and their significance in your life is the Career Center. (If you intend to transfer to a four-year school on the way to your career, remember to see Sharon Price.)

Career Assessment and Training Center

The counseling in Student Development Services continues across the sidewalk in the Career Center, the windowed area in the middle of Dogwood first floor. Norma Dawson, counselor and Career Center coordinator, began her college career at WCC and continued through graduate school before returning to the campus as a counselor. She sometimes shares with students funny but significant memories of her greatest distractions as a WCC student; she too has really "been there" and can give you some good advice. Her field of expertise is career counseling. She participates in annual workshops through the North Carolina Department of Labor to be prepared with the latest and best advice for you. (For example, the fact that North Carolina is no longer considered a *manufacturing* state but is now a *services* state is a vital factor in the career plans of North Carolina students. Did you know that the average person changes jobs seven times in a lifetime?)

The Career Center offers interest inventories, personality surveys such as the Myers-Briggs Type Indicator, "Choices" (a computer system that matches jobs with what you want in a job and the skills needed for that job), *North Carolina Careers* (a publication with specific details on job availability, training level, salary range, and employment opportunities in this state), a career resource guide called *Occupational Outlook Handbook*, college catalogs you can check out, assistance with resumes and cover letters as well as interview preparation, and one-on-one career counseling. The Career Center also offers CLEP testing.

Don't miss the great **free** opportunity to investigate your future in the Career Center. What you learn about yourself there can help you make wise academic choices at WCC.

Norma Dawson speaks to almost every ACA 111 section, so you will meet her soon.

Job Referral, Jump Start, and CO-OP Office

Leaving the Career Center, take two right turns, and on your left find yet another office filled with helpful people and resources for your future.

Anne Millington coordinates CO-OP, Jump Start, and Job Referral in Dogwood 135. She often speaks to ACA 111 classes and even teaches a section sometimes. Cooperative Education allows academic credit for approved employment, an earn-while-you-learn situation that often leads to a permanent job. You can enter this program after one semester at WCC and can use the hours to fulfill elective hours. Check your curriculum requirements in the catalog; some programs include a mandatory co-op.

Lorie Waller is the Job Referral Coordinator in Dogwood 134. She works with area employers helping them to find qualified students to fill positions. Lorie is a WCC graduate who completed her undergraduate degree in English and her master's degree in Adult Education at East Carolina University; just as several other former students have done, she eventually returned to WCC as a staff member. Placing your name in the Job Referral file in this office gives the staff a pool of students to consider when local employers call for temporary or permanent employee suggestions.

This office also coordinates two other programs: the Jump Start program for high school students eligible to take college courses and the Apprenticeship program, which offers curriculum development for industries.

Watch for announcements of Career Day in the LC Atrium. Representatives from numerous organizations and industries offer first-hand information that may influence your future!

Have you ever heard of *kaizen* (pronounced ky'zen)? It is a Japanese term for "continuous improvement," or "the relentless quest for a better way" (Pritchett 42). It appears on a list of thirteen work habits for job success in today's information-oriented society. Being in college suggests that you believe in *kaizen*; staying in college will reinforce that image; being a lifelong learner will make it possible to survive and excel in a changing world. Ask for help in your quest for a better future.

If you remain in this area after you have reached your current goals at WCC, you may want to use the services of the Office of Continuing Education and Workforce Preparedness such as the Business and Industry/Small Business Center. Remember to let WCC continue to serve you in the community.

The Foundation

The Foundation of Wayne Community College has its office in the same area of Dogwood as Job Referral and Co-Op. Associate Vice President Jack Kannan is Executive Director, and his assistant is Public Information Officer Tara Humphries. The Foundation generates scholarship funding for students and involves the community in the life of the college. Read about Foundation scholarships in Chapter 10 and about special events sponsored by the Foundation in Chapter 13. This organization enhances the life of the college as well as the life of the whole community.

Help! Security!

The Campus Security staff headed by Chief Wayne Street willingly help with everything from dead batteries to keys locked in cars, but their most important function is to keep both you and the campus safe and secure. The security force is on duty twenty-four hours a day, seven days a week. Security offers several major tips for safety:

- NEVER LEAVE YOUR BOOKS UNATTENDED, EVEN FOR SHORT PERIODS.

- Always lock your vehicle. Do not leave anything of value in sight in your vehicle.

- Avoid walking alone on campus at night. Use well-lighted areas. Security monitors parking areas as carefully as possible at dismissal times for night classes and will escort you to your car if you wish.

- Always designate the front main entrance (the one with the flags) of LC Building as your pick-up spot if you wait for a ride. (This provides shelter as well as safety.)

Directly behind the switchboard in the front of LC Building, Room 140, is the office of Campus Security. Lost and Found is located in that office; if you find a lost item on campus, please take it there, and if you lose something, check there first to see if someone else has turned it in. In May, Security gives items to Student Activities, Academic Skills Center and Salvation Army. Valuables go to the Comptroller.

Security is in charge of emergency evacuations and drills. Announcements are made through the public address system. All evacuations are real except fire drills. Instructors know the various warning signals and evacuation routes. Always evacuate in a swift and orderly fashion, taking valuables with you and moving all the way to the designated area. Special EVAC-CHAIRS are available on upper floors to accommodate people who use wheelchairs in the event of fire when elevators cannot be used.

Security also handles parking violations. All unmarked spaces belong to students. Do not park in spaces designated for visitors, staff, or handicapped. Parking stickers are available when you pay your tuition and have your i.d. card made. Display your sticker as instructed. For a temporary parking pass, contact Security through the switchboard. Your first parking violation receives a warning ticket, but subsequent violations involve a fine of $5.00. Campus-wide speed limit is 20 miles per hour. Speeding and careless and reckless driving do **not** result in mere warning tickets.

Report anyone suspected of illegal activity to Security. The SGA offers a reward of up to $100 for information that helps in the apprehension of anyone committing illegal acts on campus.

Your *Student Handbook* defines your rights and responsibilities as a student. Any act illegal off campus (theft, destruction of property, or possession of illegal drugs, for example) is also illegal on campus. Drug dogs and local law enforcement officials patrol campus periodically. Your rights as a citizen of the United States and the state of North Carolina extend to the campus unless otherwise prohibited by law; for example, no weapons are allowed on college campuses. This law includes weapons stored in vehicles.

You can reach Security through the switchboard by dialing 0 on campus or 735-5151 off campus. Notice the emergency phones in elevators and most hallways on campus; dial 250 to reach Security on the emergency phones, which have clear instructions to help a frightened or nervous caller. Dial 911 in medical emergencies. To reach Security after 9:30 on weeknights and all hours on the weekend, dial 735-5152, ext. 250. All parking lots have emergency call boxes. Look for a blue light with a decal on the pole where a call box is located.

Chief Street has requested that you read the following legal statement:

In 1990, The Campus Security Act was signed into law. The implications of the law affects, to some extent, all post secondary institutions. More importantly it involves the entire campus community, not just the campus security department in responding to crime incidents that occur on campus. In 1998, the Campus Security Act was amended and renamed The Jeanne Clery Disclosure of Campus Security Policy and Campus Crime Statistics Act. The Act requires WCC to prepare and distribute to all current faculty, staff, and students an annual report which sets forth our policies on crime prevention issues and provides statistics on the number of specific, violent crimes (murder & non-negligent manslaughter & negligent manslaughter, forcible & non-forcible sexual offenses, robbery, aggravated assault, burglary, arson, motor vehicle thefts, and hate crimes) which have occurred on campus and also the number of arrests on campus for liquor law violations, drug law violations, and weapons possessions. The annual report is available at http://www.wayne. cc.nc.us/newspub/securityreport/index.htm and printed copies are available from the security department.

HELP, another big four-letter word at WCC, is yours for the asking. Ask!

(Special thanks to staff members in all these helping areas for their many presentations to ACA 111 classes)

The Admissions and Records Office

You have successfully completed the admissions part of your dealings with the Office of Admissions and Records unless you take a break and need to go back through the admissions process. However, your relationship with this office will affect you for a long time. Registration for every semester, midterm and final grade reports, academic probation reports (try for none of those!), and transcripts for prospective employers or schools you may transfer to are just some of the procedures and documents this office generates. Your relationship precedes your first enrollment here and will continue long past your final semester because your file will stay safe and accessible here in Admissions and Records, LC 109.

The "open door" admissions policy of the North Carolina Community College System does not extend to the Health Occupations programs (Associate Degree Nursing, Practical Nursing, Dental Assisting, Dental Hygiene, Medical Assisting Technology, Dialysis Technology, and Phlebotomy). These programs, which can admit only a certain number of students each year, have additional requirements because of their limited admission status. See the catalog for the specific additional requirements.

Admissions and Records oversees the following policies and procedures that affect you:

Grading System and Calculating Your GPA

WCC uses the 4.00 grade point system: *A* earns 4 grade points per semester hour, *B* earns 3, *C* earns 2, *D* earns 1, and *F* and *WF* earn no grade points. The individual academic divisions determine the use of the seven-point scale or the ten-point scale. Instructors usually discuss the grading scale at the first class and explain it in the course handout. (Please notice that the so-called seven-point scale actually offers *eight* chances for an *A* if the scale is 93–100, for a *B* if 85–92, and for a *D* if 70–77. This scale, of course, offers 69 chances for an *F*, but you don't want to take advantage of that broad range! Similarly, the ten-point scale includes *eleven* chances for an *A* if 90–100 but *ten* if 91–100.) Study your course handouts carefully and ask your instructor early if you have questions about the grading scale.

Calculate your grade point average at the end of the semester by dividing the total number of grade points earned by the total number of semester hours attempted.

GPA = grade points earned divided by semester hours attempted. Example:

Course	Hours	Grade	Grade pts./hr.		Points earned
MAT 161	3	B	3	=	9
ENG 111	3	C	2	=	6
HIS 121	3	A	4	=	12
PED 130	1	B	3	=	3
BIO 111	4	C	2	=	8
ACA 111	1	P	0	=	0
	15				**38**

Do not include the ACA 111 in your total hours because it is a pass/fail course. Divide 38 grade points earned by 14 hours attempted. This student earns a 2.714 GPA for the semester, a very respectable record for a rather heavy schedule!

Suppose a student has more difficulty in the first semester:

MAT 161	3	D	1	=	3
ENG 111	3	C	2	=	6
PED 130	1	C	2	=	2
HIS 121	3	C	2	=	6
BIO 111	4	F	0	=	0
ACA 111	1	P	0	=	0
	15				**17**

This time you must include the 4 hours for the failed class in the number of hours attempted. Divide the 17 grade points earned by the 14 hours attempted (again excluding your ACA 111.) This student earns a 1.214 GPA. Pulling that average up to the 2.0 required for graduation will require quite an effort. Maintaining a 2.0 or higher GPA throughout your college career eliminates much of the pressure associated with graduation.

Admissions and Records staff members urge you to keep track of your grade reports and to examine them carefully for accuracy because computers and human beings together can make errors.

Credit by Examination

Credit by examination is a rather uncommon grade which requires a departmental examination, an application processed through the Office of Admissions and Records, and payment of tuition at the normal rate per hour of credit. The grade is recorded as X. The hours count toward graduation but not toward GPA.

Auditing Classes

For pleasure or review and with the instructor's permission, a student may audit a class provided space is available in the classroom. The blue audit card cannot be processed until after the first class meeting to make sure all credit students have spaces. The instructor determines whether the auditing student participates in class discussion, takes tests, and turns in other assignments or simply observes. The grade of *AU* involves no credit hours or grade points. Full-time students may audit at no extra cost; others must pay the normal hourly tuition. Credit by exam is not an option after auditing.

Graduation Requirements

The magic number is 2.0! This GPA in your major is a basic requirement for graduation from WCC. (It is also the minimum college transfer requirement, and many four-year schools will not accept any grade lower than a C. Some four-year programs demand a GPA much higher than the basic 2.0, so stay in touch with our College Transfer office and with your chosen four-year school as well once you are sure where you intend to go from here.)

Other graduation requirements are completion of all required and elective courses and minimum reading requirements in your program, clearing of all financial obligations to the college, processing of an application for graduation (watch CAMNET for the deadline), and attendance at graduation (or official permission not to attend).

Review the catalog often to stay familiar with graduation requirements in general (see "Requirements for Graduation" in your catalog) and with your specific requirements (remember the earlier advice about marking your program description pages in your catalog). Accept the responsibility for meeting these requirements. Your academic advisor knows your requirements and has computer access to your graduation readiness summary. Nevertheless, you have only *your* requirements to think about while your advisor has *many* advisees to assist and oversee.

The best way to keep track of your requirements is to use the Curriculum Guidelines form available from your advisor. Each program has its own specialized form showing graduation requirements. The General Education Core (required hours in each subject area such as humanities/fine arts, math, or social sciences) and the remaining elective hours appear in an easy-to-follow format. A list of courses fulfilling those requirements appears on the back of the Curriculum Guidelines form. You should pay careful attention to this form each time you plan your schedule for the next semester.

The Curriculum Guidelines form is also important for students planning to transfer. The Comprehensive Articulation Agreement with the UNC system determines which courses will transfer. Such courses have an identifying sentence at the end of their course descriptions in the catalog indicating that they have been approved for transfer.

Another detail to check as you plan ahead is the list of semesters in parentheses at the end of each course description in the catalog. For example, the parenthetical note after the description of MAT 272 (Sp.) indicates that Calculus II is offered only in the spring. The note after MAT 161, however, shows that College Algebra is offered every term, Fall, Spring, and Summer (F., Sp., S.).

Your advisor can help you with all of these important details. Another person you need to see if you plan to transfer before or after receiving your degree is the College Transfer Counselor, Sharon Price, in LC 114. With her help you can be sure that you are choosing the proper courses to satisfy your particular four-year school.

Schedules of students who test out of any requirements must reflect that those requirements have been met.

Registration Procedures

Study your requirements in the catalog carefully along with the tabloid listing course offerings. As advised earlier, note the evening course offerings and the WCC course offerings at Seymour Johnson Air Force Base. (Always note the dates of the base classes, which do not coincide precisely with the on-campus scheduling.) The college considers 15–17 hours a normal course load. To be considered a full-time student, you must register for at least 12 hours. You will need the signature of Dr. Dan Krautheim, Vice President for Academic Affairs, if you register for more than 20 hours. If you work more than 20 hours a week, the college recommends a part-time course load; if you register for a full-time load, consider limiting your job to 10–15 hours a week.

Telephone Registration

Preregistration is the surest way to get the schedule you want and need, and telephone registration is the easiest way to preregister. WCC students have enjoyed TRY (Telephone Registration for You) since 1996. They have experienced none of the phone registration problems often heard about on larger university campuses.

You will learn by mail when students in your major can begin to preregister by phone. The opening time is usually midnight, so be by the phone to dial at one second after midnight on your date! The order of majors rotates each semester so that students in every major eventually get first choice.

Advisors have a list of PINs (personal identification numbers for computer access) for their advisees. The PIN changes each semester, so you must see your advisor to get your PIN. Of course, you will need to see your advisor anyway to plan your schedule and coordinate your program requirements. The TRY work sheet includes the special phone number for telephone registration, which is not the regular college number, as well as step-by-step instructions for calling in on a touch tone phone. TRY continues through the last day of classes.

On-Campus Preregistration and Registration

Even before telephone registration became available, the registration process had become much simpler with the opportunity to register within the advisor's department. (The line to each departmental secretary's desk is far shorter than the line in the LC Atrium under the old system when all students processed their registration in Admissions and Records. Dr. Wilson, your college president, does not believe in making students stand in line!) If you do not register by phone, see your advisor to prepare your trial schedule card. Having several alternatives already chosen from the tabloid makes your conference with your advisor much easier. (Be sure to fill the first three blocks on the left with the course prefix such as *ENG*, course number such as *111*, and section number such as *03*. The section number is *crucial* because it distinguishes one section of a course from all other sections by the time, room and instructor. For on-campus registration or preregistration, remember to have your advisor initial beside any course that has a prerequisite to verify that you have met that prerequisite by placement test score or by having taken the previous course.)

You and your academic advisor should work together to find the most appropriate courses and schedule for you. Your advisor will check the closed course list on the computer terminal to complete your preparation. Then, unless you have received notice of an outstanding balance on the college books or of a missing item such as a transcript in your record, you can go directly from your academic advisor's office to the nearby office of the departmental secretary who will process your registration at the computer terminal. If you have received such notice, you must register at the Admissions and Records window. Pay your tuition at the Cashier's window in the LC Atrium by the designated deadline (last day of exams for preregistered students, day of registration for others). **Remember to pay your tuition (or go to Cashier's window for instructions if you have a Pell Grant) or your preregistration will be worthless!**

Take the schedule that you receive when you pay your tuition to all of your classes at the beginning of the semester. Then if for some reason your name does not appear on the roster, you will have the proof the instructor needs to allow you in the class.

Registration Changes

If you wish to change your registration, you must process the addition or other change on an orange card with your advisor's signature through the Office of Admissions and the Business Office by the last day to add a class (see the calendar list near the front of your catalog or check your *Student Handbook*). The last day to drop a class without failing is always the 51st day of the semester (see calendar). Withdrawing from the college completely means officially dropping all classes; in that case, the grade for each class will be *W*.

Attendance Policy

Several other sections in this book address the attendance policy: a student who has absences exceeding 20 percent of the scheduled class sessions will receive a *W* if the student exceeds the limit before the last day to drop and a *WF* if after the last day to drop. Monitor your attendance carefully. Be aware of any departmental tardiness policies affecting the number of absences. Late registration produces unexcused absences. Register before classes begin unless you have an unavoidable conflict; missing the first class does *not* make a good beginning.

NOTE: The 20% attendance policy may have been changed to a smaller percentage by the time you read this.

Tuition, Residence Classification, and Refunds

Did you know that North Carolina has the lowest community college tuition in the nation except in Texas? The state legislature determines tuition.

Check your catalog for current tuition and fees, residence classification for tuition, and refund policies. Knowing the deadlines for tuition refunds can save you much money if you have to drop any classes or withdraw from school.

If you drop before the class begins, you will receive a full refund. If you drop on or before the 10 percent point, you will receive a 75 percent refund.

Midterm Grade Reports

Check the calendar in your *Student Handbook* and the calendar list in your catalog for *midterm* each semester. Very soon after that date, instructors issue midterm reports for any students in danger of failing. The Office of Admissions and Records then mails midterm reports to every student identified by instructors. The report lists all courses the student is enrolled in and shows an *M* beside the course or courses the student is having trouble with. The *M* warning is just that, a warning or wake-up call. Some students who receive midterm reports end the semester with an excellent grade; some do indeed fail; some choose after consulting with instructor and advisor to withdraw by the last day to drop so receive a grade of *W* on the final grade report at the end of the semester. The grade of *M* is only a temporary grade; it does not remain on the record after the end of the semester.

Arriving within days after midterm, the midterm report gives students ample time to seek help from instructors, counselors, and the many facilities described in the "Help!" chapter. If you ever get a midterm report, consider it an opportunity to make a good decision about whether to tackle your difficult course with renewed force or to withdraw from it and concentrate on your other courses for the remainder of the semester. To withdraw, go to the Admissions and Records window to process an orange card initialed by your instructor and signed by your advisor; be sure to talk to your instructor and your advisor before making your final decision. (Students sometimes ask a different instructor to initial or sign a drop card, but in fairness to your instructor, your advisor, and especially yourself, you should consult your own instructor and your own advisor. You should know where and when both your instructor and your advisor are available, and you can certainly schedule an appointment if those times are not convenient for you. "Let your right hand know what your left hand is doing" applies to this situation; your advisor and instructor can do their jobs better if they know your intentions.)

Final Grade Reports

Instructors usually must turn in final grades no later than 9:00 A.M. on the day after exams end. Students receive grades in the mail within a few days. The final grade report includes the grade for each course, the grade point average for that semester, and the cumulative grade point average. (Instructors do not report exam grades to the Office of Admissions and Records. Grade books remain on file in the various academic departments.) **Always notify Admissions and Records of address changes.** Do not depend on yellow or orange registration cards; go to Admissions and Records to process a change of address form.

President's List and Dean's List

The college acknowledges outstanding academic achievement with two prestigious lists. The President's List recognizes students who earn a GPA of 4.0 while enrolled in at least twelve semester hours. The Dean's List recognizes students who earn a GPA of 3.60 with no grade lower than C while enrolled in at least twelve semester hours. (A grade of *Incomplete* excludes a student from these lists.) The local newspaper publishes the lists, and students earning these honors receive letters of congratulations from the college.

Confidentiality of Student Records

The Office of Admissions and Records maintains student records on file in a secure setting. The catalog identifies the only circumstances under which access to these records is permitted based on the Family Educational Rights and Privacy Act of 1974. If you prefer that the college not release even basic directory information about you to anyone, you must notify the Office of Admissions and Records and sign a request. (Directory information: name, major, dates of attendance, degrees and awards.)

Academic Progress

Effective Fall 1995, the college implemented a new policy designed to help you maintain satisfactory progress and complete your program successfully at WCC. Students who do not maintain the prescribed academic progress toward the 2.0 required for completion of their programs will receive notice of academic probation from the Office of Admissions and Records and must consult with their academic advisors to discuss options for assistance. They must subsequently demonstrate progress by achieving a 2.0 each semester of the probationary period. Students who do not demonstrate such progress must reduce their academic course load, continue under probationary status for the next semester, transfer to another curriculum, or be suspended for one semester. (Individual determination of option will apply to each affected student.) Prolonged academic difficulty has very adverse effects on financial aid and veterans' benefits as well as on general academic success.

Transcript Requests

You must request in writing to have an official transcript sent to another institution. You do not have to pay to have the first transcript sent, but subsequent transcripts require a fee of one dollar, a real bargain compared to fees at other schools.

Transcript requests will probably be one of your long-term ties to WCC. For the remainder of your academic and professional life, the Office of Admissions and Records at WCC will be here for you whenever you need a transcript sent to another school or workplace!

Questions?

Someone from Admissions and Records will probably speak to your ACA 111 class and answer any questions you may have.

(Many thanks to Susan Sasser, Director of Admissions and Records, for advice on the information to include in this chapter, and to Ms. Sasser, Dianne Allgaier, and Yvonne Robbins for their many presentations in ACA 111 classes)

Diversity and Culture: More Learning Opportunities

Most college graduates would include on a list of the most important lessons learned in college many that did not come from a classroom. Exposure to a variety of people and viewpoints constitutes a significant part of education, a process that never ends.

Answer the following questions based on a self-assessment in *Right from the Start: Managing Your Way to College Success* (Holkeboer 11.2):

Do most of your friends come from the same background as you do?____

Are you trying to be open-minded even though you have some prejudices?____

Have you been inside the United States all your life?____

Is English the only language you have studied?____

Do you expect not to find prejudice on a college campus?____

Do you feel uncomfortable around foreign students?____

Do you feel awkward around people with disabilities (someone who uses a wheelchair, for example)?____

Do you ever feel any prejudice is directed against you?____

Do you think people should be good sports and accept ethnic jokes or jokes that make fun of certain people?____

Are you satisfied with your cultural attitudes and see no reason to change them?____

Do you think women and men have equal opportunities in the United States?____

Did you answer *yes* to more than five statements?____ *Please read on.*

The terms "multicultural" and "cultural diversity" may evoke images of "We Are the World" or childhood memories of "Jesus loves the little children. . . . Red and yellow, black and white," but the word *culture* involves much more than international variety. What does being part of a *culture* mean to you?

_____

_____

_____

_____

_____

Does your answer include something about being part of a group with shared traditions and values?

Name three cultures that include you.

_____   _____   _____

Does your list include your gender? Your age group? What about race? Religious background? National origin? Ethnic background? Lifestyle? Socioeconomic group? Educational background? Learning style? What about your physical capabilities or a physical challenge you may have? (Even the term "physically challenged" represents a new attitude and a new awareness, not merely of PC, or political correctness, but of sensitivity in our use of language; the old term "handicap" has negative connotations for many people.)

In this class you may meet Spanish and French instructor Fe Finch or see her Powerpoint presentation on diversity. The story of her family's flight from Cuba after Castro's revolution in 1961 is fascinating, and she is particularly adept at offering colleagues and students some challenging ideas about race, culture, and diversity. She emphasizes that the details most often associated with race such as skin color, hair texture, or physical features do not determine race; the genetic factors that do determine race may surprise you. What makes a person Hispanic is another commonly misunderstood concept. Enhancing your own awareness of racial and cultural identity is a part of a true education.

Human beings tend to consider their own group "best." That attitude is sometimes called *ethnocentric*. The college community gives students who have grown up in a very homogeneous culture, one in which everybody is very much alike, a chance to meet people from a variety of backgrounds. That opportunity can lead to understanding and respect for people who are not just like you. Coming to accept them with their differences, to feel comfortable around them, to incorporate ideas from their cultures into your own—this kind of growth leads to *multiculturalism* (Holkeboer 11.16).

Look around your orientation class. Do you see people much younger or much older than you? What other differences do you see? How many different ways could you divide the group? Name three ways.

_____

_____

_____

Now look again. List at least two things that you all have in common.

_____

_____

Suprisingly, one small ACA 111 class in the spring of 2000 had **five** New York natives in it!

Your instructor may give you time to pair off and learn a few more characteristics you share with someone who appears very different. Walt Whitman's "Song of Myself" begins with a celebration of self but immediately identifies self with everyone else in the world, recognizing that all human beings are in this thing called life together: "I celebrate myself, and sing myself, / And what I assume you shall assume, / For every atom belonging to me as good belongs to you."

Recognizing your shared concerns, problems, joys, hopes, and goals (and remembering that, like Tennyson's Ulysses, you are a part of all that you have met) can be a milestone in your own journey to become the most complete human being you can possibly be. After all, isn't that part of why you came to college?

SGA has a standing committee for Special Populations. Its chairperson is responsible for planning student activities that reaffirm WCC's policy as an Equal Opportunity/Affirmative Action college. The Diversity Task Force celebrates Black History Month in February, Women's History Month in March, and variety all year.

Watch for special events advertised, and become a part of the celebration of diversity. For a real education that never stops, take advantage of every way that a college campus reflects the world.

Cultural Opportunities in College

Another meaning of *culture* is addressed in one of the purposes of Wayne Community College: to improve the cultural level of students and community. An institution of higher learning has a responsibility for enhancing the quality of life in its community by offering intellectual stimulation and exposure to the arts. The college campus is an appropriate setting for concerts, lectures, plays, and forums.

Moffatt Auditorium in the LC Building has been the setting for impressive events. Pulitzer Prize nominee and National Book Award winner Tim O'Brien spoke there. Wambui Bahati performed *Balancing Act*, her one-woman musical on bipolar disorder. Robin Voiers gave a one-woman portrayal of Margaret Sanger, birth control pioneer. A group of North Carolina writers including humanities instructor Margaret Baddour presented a Readers' Theater; two of the visiting writers, Joseph Bathanti and Jaki Shelton Green, gave guest lectures in classes.

The Foundation of WCC makes such campus events possible and also helps to sponsor performances by groups like the National Opera Company at the Paramount Theater. WCC students can attend all of these events absolutely free. Executive Director of the Foundation Jack Kannan has led in the creation of an Arts and Humanities Program with its own director, William Brettmann, who organizes special seminars and trips for campus and community. Goldsboro native William Stone, an internationally renowned opera singer, starred in a gala fundraiser for the Foundation in March of 2001 and gave a master class which WCC students could observe at no cost.

The Foundation also sponsors drama productions featuring students, faculty, staff, and community actors. Since the late eighties, the following plays have been produced: *We the People, Our Town* (twice), *Inherit the Wind*, a Shakespeare Festival in the amphitheatre, *On Golden Pond, Da, Home, Lion in Winter, A Christmas Carol* (twice), *Shadowlands, An Evening with Oscar Wilde, Love Letters, Woman in Black*, and *A Man for All Seasons*. A joint production with James Sprunt Community College was *Spoon River Anthology*, performed on both campuses and at Okracoke. In the spring of 2001, more than 1500 people saw the WCC production of *Macbeth*.

The 2001–2003 college calendar promises several theatre opportunities for students. Broaden your horizons—see some plays. Better still, audition and *be in a play*!

Music students of the Liberal Arts Division perform in concerts and at graduation. Art students show their work in the Atrium. Drama students perform and direct scenes and brief productions. Fashion Merchandising students give shows and exhibit their work in the library.

The Multi-Cultural Association for Enrichment sponsors a Martin Luther King, Jr., Celebration with a motivational speaker followed by a Soul Food Banquet. Regular meetings of the International Students' Club feature presentations by students on the customs of their homelands. All students are welcome at these events. An outlet for students' own creativity is *Renaissance*, the campus literary magazine, which welcomes submissions of poetry, essays, short stories, and art.

Many instructors arrange field trips related to courses. Bentonville Battleground, Wayne County History Museum, North Carolina Museum of Art, North Carolina Shakespeare Festival, Playmakers Theater, the Royal Tea Rooms, a demonstration of the pipe organ at First Presbyterian Church, a lecture by feminist Gloria Steinem, *The Washington Post* in the nation's capital—you may find yourself with a class at any of those places—or even at a hog farm! Instructors will also keep you informed about cultural events in the area.

Goldsboro and Wayne County actively support the arts. The Arts Council sponsors a variety of interest groups such as Goldsboro Ballet, Center Stage Theater, Stagestruck (young people's theater), a North Carolina Symphony chapter, Wayne Community Concerts Association (free to students with WCC i.d.), Third Century Singers, Cultural Movement (African dancers), Buck Swamp Kickin' Cloggers, Writers' Group, African American Arts Association, and a photography group, as well as an art gallery which sponsors a Juried Art Show that attracts artists nationwide. Many faculty, staff, and students are involved in these groups, and art instructor Patricia Turlington and several of her students have been recognized in the Juried Art Show.

You may have an extra credit opportunity for attending various community arts events; English instructors sometimes give credit for written responses to these performances. Students often express their gratitude to instructors for making them aware of a whole side of the community that they had missed before enrolling at WCC.

Some of you may be wondering, "What does all this cultural opportunity stuff have to do with *my* major?" A journalist named Paul O'Connor addresses that question with a stirring response to a high school student who asked then-Governor Jim Hunt why a kid who wants to be a TV repairman is required to read Shakespeare. O'Connor says he would have answered the boy's question this way:

"Son, we have you read Shakespeare because you are here for more than job training. You are here to be taught about life. When you read *Romeo and Juliet*, you will learn about love and romance and the joy and pain they can cause. When you read *Hamlet* and *Macbeth*, you will learn of good and evil, of deception and treachery. *Much Ado About Nothing* will show you how silly we can all be, and how appearance and reality can differ.

"When you go beyond Shakespeare and read other great writers, you will learn of courage from Homer and of good and evil from Dante. From Twain's *Huckleberry Finn*, you will learn about friendship, and from Fitzgerald's *The Great Gatsby*, you will learn about dreams.

Young man, our society requires more than good TV repairmen—in fact it might be better served by poor repairmen who leave us without the infernal boxes for a few nights. Our society requires good and moral citizens, people who can love and dream and take care of their young.

"We need a society that shares common values. Those values, I say sadly, are missing today in much of our society. The proof of that rests in our crime statistics. When your teacher assigns our great writers, she is introducing you to the western set of values that evolved over thousands of years.

"If we teach you those values, and your life is full and satisfying regardless of your material standing, then I'd say we've done our job.

"That's why students who aspire to be TV repairmen need to read Shakespeare." (4A)

Former WCC President G. Herman Porter is among the many people who have published articles about the value of a liberal arts education. Medical schools have come to recognize that the humanities enhance the education of physicians. No matter what your major is, exposure to a variety of art forms and to intellectually exciting presentations on diverse topics adds a special dimension to your education at WCC. Seize every opportunity to broaden your horizons, to educate the whole person that you are or want to be. *Carpe diem!*

(Thanks to Fe Finch, Wade Hallman, Annette Hawkins and the Diversity Task Force, and the WCC Foundation)

Tips from Former Students

- Take College Student Success first. *Congratulations if you are following this advice now!*

- ACA 111 is a very good class if you are new. Make it one of your first priorities.

- Get a map of campus. Ask for a tour from your advisor or ACA 111 instructor.

- Talk to someone in the Financial Aid office to find out what you may be eligible for.

- Find out *everything* about financial aid and *then* apply.

- Money (financial aid) is available. Take the time to find out.

- If you are applying for financial aid, make sure you find out the deadlines for both federal grants and state assistance grants.

- Learn what programs do not qualify a student for financial aid. (Basic Law Enforcement Training and Phlebotomy are two examples.)

- Remember to study hard. Remember that teachers are here to help you. Don't be afraid to ask for help.

- Get acquainted with your instructors so you can learn as much as possible and make your learning experience more enjoyable.

- Always know where instructors' offices are in case you need them. In many cases, instructors' offices are upstairs in the building where they teach most often.

- Take advantage of all the wisdom available from faculty and staff.

- Take advantage of the services that WCC offers for extra help such as tutors and Academic Skills. There is no excuse for not learning and understanding your studies.

- Be prepared for a test at least one day ahead.

- Always take notes writing clearly in case you have a notebook test.

- Listen closely to what the instructor says.

- Do not fall behind on your reading or you will regret it. It is difficult to catch up at the last minute.

- Preregister because classes fill up fast and you may not get the classes you want unless you preregister.

- See Sharon Price in LC 114 for specific college transfer advice.

- Before deciding about transferring to another college, make sure you're taking classes that will transfer.

- Learn who your advisor is and become friends with him or her.

- Stay in touch with your advisor.

- Find out what to do to get into your chosen major and what specific courses are required.

- Get a catalog that lists all your graduation requirements. *Also get a curriculum guidelines form from your advisor and keep it updated.*

- Do not register for a required class you tested out of until a semester when you are already paying for a full-time load.

- Make time to go to the Career Center to research your career plans and make sure the career you have chosen is right for you.

- Investigate the employment outlook in your chosen field.

- Use "people resources"—talk to everyone available about the college and your classes. The more information you have, the better!

- Searching the bulletin boards for used books can save you a small fortune.

- Don't be afraid to ask questions.

- Get involved. Ask questions. Everyone at WCC is human. It will make your life at WCC easier if you know all your resources. Don't be afraid.

- Be positive and confident, take control of your life, don't be scared to ask questions or get help, and most of all *try*!

- Learn the drop/add procedure.

- Learn about clubs available through Student Activities.

- Find out where things other than your classes are on campus.

- Find the library. It will be extremely helpful.

- Visit the library. Learn where everything is and how to use all the computers.

- When planning your classes, don't forget to figure in study time.

- Never copy anyone else's work. Plagiarism is against WCC rules and could get you kicked out of WCC!

- Find out some information about an instructor before signing up for that instructor's class, but get opinions from more than one student. Schedule a light load (perhaps including just one hard class) for your first semester so you can get the feel of college.

- Try to meet the instructor before signing up for the class.

- Do your studying away from the cafeteria and your friends.

- One can learn a great deal at WCC.

- Go to class!

- Come to class on time and be efficient.

- Go to class every day, and pay special attention to the instructor.

- Before coming to class, make sure you had a good night's sleep.

- Come to ACA 111 class at least 13 times out of 16 to pass!

- Make study notes and make use of the time you have between classes. Get a tutor if needed.

- Study more than you think you should.

- Find out about Basic Skills Computer Lab in Pine Building. It can help so much.

- Use the Academic Skills Center.

- The Writing Center can help you catch up on assignments.

- Take failing a test as a hint to get a tutor right away. Use all the facilities available. Don't be embarrassed.

- If a retest is available, take it.

- Join a study group.

- Always read your calendar in the *Student Handbook* to make sure you are not left out of anything.

- Learn how many slots are available if you are on a waiting list for a program like nursing.

- Learn what classes are not offered at night if you are a night student.

- Find out about Seymour Johnson classes.

- Learn how much time will be required to make a good grade in the classes you want to take.

- Voice your opinion. Someone will listen. *Use the Suggestion Box outside the Student Activities Office.*

- Be proud of your ability to go to college and succeed in your program.

- Take a chance on things you are nervous about doing.

- Don't give up.

- Have fun and study hard. Hold your head up high—you're a college student now!

Chapter Fifteen

Tips from Faculty Who Once Were Students Like You

From having been students like you themselves and from teaching other students like you, your instructors offer the following advice (in random order):

- Learn how to get up early to study in the morning.

- Begin any long-range assignment immediately. Never wait.

- Listen! (Instructors notice that some students tune out and later say, "I didn't know that.")

- Ask questions.

- Write down information.

- Be positive! No instructor likes to hear "I hate English" (or math or whatever the instructor teaches).

- In answering an essay or discussion question on a test, assume nothing. Go about answering the question as if the person you are explaining the topic to knows absolutely nothing about it. When students assume that the instructor knows what they are trying to explain, they often leave out critical concepts or information and consequently lose points on the question.

- Use note cards or flash cards for studying.

- See your advisor or instructor immediately if you do poorly on your first test. Seek help in the appropriate place such as Academic Skills Center, Writing Center, Basic Skills Computer Lab.

- Never ask an instructor if you missed anything when you were absent; of course you did! Instead, ask *what* you missed.

- Sit at or near the front of the class to screen out distractions and to make seeing and hearing easier.

- If you sit near someone who talks, move.

- College faculty expect courtesy and a mature attention span.

- Accept responsibility for the consequences of your actions.

- No matter how big or overwhelming the assignment, it can be handled if it is broken into smaller parts. Learn to think of it in its small parts. Determine how it can be broken down and then learn/complete/accomplish one part at a time. This leads to management of a once overwhelming assignment.

- Remember that there is no *I* in *TEAM*. We are all working as a team here at WCC. (An instructor heard this from a student.)

- Don't overload with courses your first semester; get used to being a student and studying. Then you will know how heavy a load you can handle.

- Let teachers know the minute you have trouble with a course. Don't be shy about asking for help. The sooner you get help, the better. Sometimes it's too late if you wait until the second half of the semester to seek help.

- Take lots of notes in all your classes. Taking notes helps you to stay alert and stay focused. Rewrite your notes when you get home. This will help you retain the information. However, don't try to write down every word; keep your phrases short.

- Learn to take good notes.

- Learn keyboarding and type all your papers on a word processor or computer.

- When I finally learned that there is no such thing as a stupid question, things got a lot easier!

- Ask your advisor for a curriculum guidelines form; then keep records of courses and grades as you complete requirements for your degree. Save all your grade mailers.

- Obtain a copy of the *Student Handbook,* and use it for marking your assignment deadlines and appointments. The calendar format makes it a good tool.

- Let your instructors know you like them—hug them!

- (Follow the preceding tip selectively!)

- If you must enter a classroom after class has begun, be courteous and walk *behind,* not in front of, the speaker. Give student presenters the same courtesy you would give the instructor.

- Develop a relationship with instructors early. Realize that they are people too and are approachable.

- Develop some system for organizing course handouts, assignment sheets, completed tests, and other course items right away so that they are always readily available for reference.

- Do not procrastinate on assignments. Complete and turn them in without undue delay. Control the assignments; don't let them control you.

- Do not miss class casually. You may have some legitimate need to miss later, and your earlier cuts will make it hard for even an understanding instructor to excuse the excessive number of absences.

- Neither avoid nor choose an instructor based solely on what other students say; form your own opinions. You may work very well with an instructor whom your friend avoids.

- Don't take the same instructor every time. (The benefits of exposure to a variety of viewpoints and styles outweigh the benefits of the comfort zone.)

- Don't get behind in math.

- If you're not an early person, sit at the back but near the door.

- Give us a break! We've heard all those excuses before!

- Don't zip your book bag or make your departure preparations until your instructor ends the class.

- Get to know the library early. Give it a chance as your study place.

- Visit the Career Center (Dogwood 120), the College Transfer Office (LC 114), and the Job Referral office (Dogwood 135) early.

- Math is not a spectator sport. It requires active participation. Have a positive attitude. Forget any negative math experiences in your earlier education. Forget anything you've been told about being "stupid" in math or that "it's in your genes and there's nothing you can do about it." Develop an "I can" and an "I will" attitude. Set your goal to make it through the course the first time. After your attitude adjustment, do what needs to be done. Math is learned by practicing, practicing, practicing. Michael Jordan didn't learn to be a great basketball player without practicing every day. Homework is a must. Before you put pencil to paper, read the material in the book and study the examples. Go back over your notes from class. As you work the problems, don't get in the habit of looking up the answer first and then working toward that answer. Do what you think needs to be done and then check. If you need extra practice on a particular type of problem, work other problems in that area until you feel comfortable with the concept. Ask the instructor to explain problems you have difficulty with, either in class or during his/her office hour. Once you finish the written assignment, read the next section to be discussed. Even if you don't understand it, you'll at least be familiar with the terminology.

- Class attendance is essential in math. The instructor can shed light on the work and let you in on some of those mathematical "tricks."

- Form study groups. Get the phone number of at least one other student in your class so you can bounce ideas off each other. If you can explain a problem to another person, you will understand it better.

- Do not put off studying for a math test until the night before. Review a little each day by working a problem or two from each section. The night before the test you should only have to review a little and then get a good night's sleep.

- Have a certain place to study at home. Use that place for nothing else besides studying. (Your body will get the message.)

- Make sure your advisor gets to know you. (Advisors want to know their advisees.)

- Keep in mind that your instructors are not miracle workers. They can point you in the right direction, but you have to take the next steps. They will be there to help you if you stumble. Ask for help.

- At the beginning of the semester, study your schedule carefully to determine the days your classes meet. A common blunder on any campus is showing up for a Monday/Wednesday/Friday class on Tuesday if classes begin on Tuesday! (You may even catch an instructor doing this.) Keep your schedule handy.

- Pay your tuition on time if you preregister so you won't lose your classes!

- Plant your corn early!

- Take advantage of all the cultural experiences available.

- Accept your responsibilities as a student. English instructor Gerald Simmons provides each of his students a copy of a document borrowed from Lynne Marie Rodell of Christian Brothers University in Tennessee, "English Anxiety Bill of Responsibilities." It reminds students of the following responsibilities: Go to class and behave appropriately. Prepare for class using textbook and notes. Seek help when needed. Realize that the teacher is not responsible for making students understand and learn. View the teacher not as an enemy but as a partner. Behave as an adult. Be courteous. Expect to be evaluated by the same standards demanded of all other students.

- Read CAMNET often!

- Because it attempts to be as current and practical as possible, this textbook always will include changing details. Be alert to these. However, the basic concept does not change. YOU ARE HERE, and WCC IS HERE FOR YOU with unbelievable opportunities. Seize the day!

Thanks to all (in alphabetical order) who responded to the call for tips: Mable Almond, Marie Barnes, Bill Bennett, Faye Best, Tim Brewer, Sharon Bull, Linda Chitty, Paul Compton, Anna Edmundson, Liz Meador, Phyllis Patterson, Diane Price, Doug Royal, Gerald Simmons, Betty Jo Slozak, Kathryn Spicer, Miriam Wessell, Marian Westbrook, Peggy Womble.

Chapter Sixteen

Success Ahead

Especially to Evening Students

To say that the college can offer you everything it offers day students would not be completely truthful.

Wayne Community College is not an evening school. However, many recent changes and improvements reflect the college's commitment to you. Richard Harris, Evening Coordinator, is available in LC 136 from 4:00 P.M. till 10:00 P.M. Monday–Thursday. The course offerings are increasing. Admissions and Records, Financial Aid, and Student Development observe evening hours (5:00–7:00) on a rotating basis; the schedule is announced on CAMNET. Several facilities on campus such as the library, computer labs, and Writing Center now have regular Saturday hours, hoping you can benefit from those. Security makes a special effort to be available when night classes end.

For several years now, evening ACA 111 students have had the unique opportunity of an hour with the president. Dr. Ed Wilson made a voluntary commitment to visit night College Student Success classes every semester. He listens and follows up on requests, questions, suggestions, or complaints presented by students. In fact, he credits former evening students with the ideas for many improvements. (He also graciously accepts the compliments many students pay the college!)

Most instructors cofess to a special love for night classes. Instructors and students alike are tired, for most have already worked all day, so you have something in common right away. However, the level of motivation compensates for the fatigue. You are a special breed of students. Keep up the good work—SUCESS AHEAD!

Carpe diem!

How frustrating to end a book recognizing the impossibility of telling you "everything you need to know about WCC" even *almost* everthing you need to know about WCC." Why don't YOU finish the book? Please use the following pages to add your own tips and tidbits. Tear it out and turn it in to your instructor the last day of class. Then the new students who come after you can benefit from your discoveries about the campus and about college.

Because everything you need to know cannot be packed into one small book any more than it can be packed into sixteen class sessions, one goal of this course and of this book is AWARENESS. Please list three things you are aware of now because you read this book and took this course that you were not aware of the first day of the semester.

1. _____

_____

2. _____

_____

3. _____

_____

Perhaps the best thing you could have learned is how much more there is to learn at Wayne Community College.

Squeeze all you can get out of WCC, out of life, out of yourself! Become all you can become. Seize the day!

Now—on with the challenges and rewards of college and life! SUCCESS AHEAD!

Enjoy!

Tips for the Next New Students

_____

_____

_____

_____

_____

_____

_____

_____

_____

_____

_____

_____

Chapter Fifteen

Sources Cited

American Academy of Otolaryngology—Head and Neck Surgery, Inc. *Secondhand Smoke and Children*. Alexandria, Va. 1998.

Barkley, Susan E. "Community Building." *Innovation Abstracts* 23.14 (April 27, 2001): 1–2.

Carter, Carol, and Sarah Lyman Kravits. *Keys to Success: How to Achieve Your Goals*. Upper Saddle River, NJ: Prentice Hall, 1996.

Ellis, David B. *Becoming A Master Student*. 7th ed. Boston: Houghton, 1994.

Epidemiology and Special Studies Branch of the North Carolina Department of Environment, Health, and Natural Resources. *1998 HIV/AIDS Surveillance Report*.

Hartman, Neal A. *Fresh Perspectives*. Dubuque, Iowa: Kendall/Hunt, 1993.

Holkeboer, Robert. *Right from the Start: Managing Your Way to College Success*. Belmont, CA: Wadsworth, 1993.

"International Statistics." Division of HIV/AIDS Prevention, Centers for Disease Control and Prevention. Updated 2 Jan 2001. 28 May 2001 <http://www.cdc.gov/hiv/stats/internat.htm.>.

Jewler, Jerome, and John N. Gardner with Mary-Jane McCarthy, eds. *Your College Experience: Strategies for Success*. Concise Edition. The Freshman Year Experience Series. Belmont, CA: Wadsworth, 1993.

Jewler, Jerome, John N. Gardner, and Hilda F. Owens. "Keys to Success." Jewler and Gardner with McCarthy. 1–22.

Jones, Michael B. "Listen Up." *Renaissance* 15 (1999): 58.

Lawry, John D. *How to Succeed at School: Letters of A Professor to His Daughter*. Kansas City, MO: Sheed and Ward, 1988.

Long, Kenneth N., and Debora A. Ritter. "Making the Grade." Jewler and Gardner with McCarthy. 93–116.

Maxwell, Martha. "Are the Skills We Are Teaching Obsolete? A Review of Recent Research in Reading and Study Skills." *Research in Developmental Education* 10.5 (1993): 1–4.

Mohn, Lisa Ann, N. Peter Johnson, Preston E. Johnson, and Kevin W. King. "Healthy Decisions: Sexuality, Drugs, and Stress." Jewler and Gardner with McCarthy. 211–240.

North Carolina. N. C. AIDS Advisory Council. *The 2000 North Carolina AIDS Index*. AIDS Care Branch, 2000.

O'Connor, Paul T. "Job Training Isn't Enough." *Goldsboro* [NC] *News-Argus* 7 Sept 1993:4A.

Peck, M. Scott. *The Road Less Traveled: A New Psychology of Love, Traditional Values and Spiritual Growth*. New York: Simon & Schuster, 1978.

Pritchett, Price. *The Employee Handbook of New Work Habits for A Radically Changing World: 13 Ground Rules for Job Success in the Information Age*. Dallas: Pritchett and Associates, 1994.

"Slant—Encouraging Participation." *Student Success: A Newsletter of College Survival*. January 1995.

U.S. Dept. of Health and Human Services. *Questions and Answers About TB*. Atlanta: Centers for Disease Control and Prevention/Division of Tuberculosis Elimination, 1994.

Walter, Timothy L., and Al Siebert. *Student Success: How to Succeed in College and Still Have Time for Your Friends*. Fort Worth: Harcourt, 1993.

Walther, Daniel R. *Toolkit for College Success*. Belmont, CA: Wadsworth, 1994.

NOTE: Additional sources include the general catalog of WCC, the security brochure, *Student Handbook*, and dozens of faculty, staff, and students.

About the Author

Rosalyn Fleming Lomax, Liberal Arts faculty member and Student Success Coordinator at Wayne Community College, teaches a variety of English classes as well as Theater Appreciation and many sections of College Student Success. She is an editor of *Renaissance,* the WCC writers' and artists' magazine. Her own days as a student resulted in a Bachelor of Arts degree in English from the University of North Carolina at Greensboro and a Master of Arts degree in English from the University of North Carolina at Chapel Hill. In 1988 she received the Excellence in Teaching Award at WCC, and in 1993 *USA Today* honored her on its top fifty list of American and Canadian community college instructors.

Her passion for students and for teaching reflects her passionate love of family, friends, faith, church, music, literature, the stage, walking, the beach, snow, and chocolate. Some students find her rather hyperactive.

Index